External Higher Education Quality Assurance in China

Since the end of the 1990s, the Chinese higher education system has seen a dramatic expansion of enrolment. China currently has the largest higher education system in the world, however, the rapid growth resulted in concerns being raised about the quality of the system. In response, an array of external quality assessment schemes of higher education has been established, based on suggested policy designs and reforms. The establishment of an effective quality assurance mechanism is a major challenge for universities around the world, therefore, what experience and lessons can be learned from the Chinese practice?

This book analyses the external quality assurance system of higher education in China. It brings together scholarship on this topic by renowned Chinese experts, reporting and discussing recent policy developments and research. It presents and analyses various quality evaluation schemes, covering undergraduate, postgraduate, and vocational levels of higher education. The theoretical roots and value orientation of Chinese higher education quality assurance are also reflected on.

This book was originally published as a special issue of *Chinese Education & Society*.

Liu Shuiyun is an associate professor in the Faculty of Education at Beijing Normal University, China. Her main research interests include higher education, quality assessment, and educational policy. She has published in a number of journals, including *Higher Education, Higher Education Policy, Educational Studies*, and *Higher Education Management and Policy*.

External Higher Education Quality Assurance in China

Edited by
Liu Shuiyun

Routledge
Taylor & Francis Group

LONDON AND NEW YORK

First published 2018
by Routledge
2 Park Square, Milton Park, Abingdon, Oxon, OX14 4RN, UK

and by Routledge
711 Third Avenue, New York, NY 10017, USA

Routledge is an imprint of the Taylor & Francis Group, an informa business

British Library Cataloguing in Publication Data
A catalogue record for this book is available from the British Library

ISBN 13: 978-1-138-56438-1

Typeset in Times New Roman
by RefineCatch Limited, Bungay, Suffolk

Publisher's Note
The publisher accepts responsibility for any inconsistencies that may have
arisen during the conversion of this book from journal articles to book chapters,
namely the possible inclusion of journal terminology.

Disclaimer
Every effort has been made to contact copyright holders for their permission to
reprint material in this book. The publishers would be grateful to hear from any
copyright holder who is not here acknowledged and will undertake to rectify
any errors or omissions in future editions of this book.

Contents

CONTENTS

vi

Citation Information

The chapters in this book were originally published in *Chinese Education & Society*, volume 49, issue 1–2 (January 2016). When citing this material, please use the original page numbering for each article, as follows:

Chapter 1
External Higher Education Quality Assurance System in China
Liu Shuiyun
Chinese Education & Society, volume 49, issue 1–2 (January 2016), pp. 1–6

Chapter 2
Quality Assurance in Higher Education: Reflection, Criticism, and Change
Zhang Yingqiang and Su Yongjian
Chinese Education & Society, volume 49, issue 1–2 (January 2016), pp. 7–19

Chapter 3
On the Effects, Problems, and Countermeasures of Undergraduate Teaching Evaluation in Higher Education
Liu Xianjun, Yu Yang, Zhang Junchao, Wei Shuguang, and Ding Ling
Chinese Education & Society, volume 49, issue 1–2 (January 2016), pp. 20–38

Chapter 4
The Effectiveness of the Higher Education Quality Assessment System: Problems and Countermeasures in China
Zhou Guangli
Chinese Education & Society, volume 49, issue 1–2 (January 2016), pp. 39–48

Chapter 5
Newly Built Undergraduate Schools Should Place Great Emphasis on Connotation Construction and Quality Promotion: An Analysis Based on the Qualification Evaluation Results for 41 Undergraduate Schools
Zhong Binglin
Chinese Education & Society, volume 49, issue 1–2 (January 2016), pp. 49–59

Chapter 6

The Value Orientation of Higher Vocational Education Evaluation: A Textual Analysis of an Evaluation Program
Wang Yonglin and Wang Zhanjun
Chinese Education & Society, volume 49, issue 1–2 (January 2016), pp. 60–71

Chapter 7

The Operation Mechanisms of External Quality Assurance Frameworks of Foreign Higher Education and Implications for Graduate Education
Lin Mengquan, Chang Kai, and Gong Le
Chinese Education & Society, volume 49, issue 1–2 (January 2016), pp. 72–85

Chapter 8

Data-Intensive Evaluation: The Concept, Methods, and Prospects of Higher Education Monitoring Evaluation
Wang Zhanjun, Qiao Weifeng, and Li Jiangbo
Chinese Education & Society, volume 49, issue 1–2 (January 2016), pp. 86–98

Chapter 9

The Evolution of Topics and Leading Trends over the Past 15 Years of Research on the Quality of Higher Education in China: Based on Keyword Co-Occurrence Knowledge Map Analysis of the Research Papers Published from 2000 to 2014 in the CSSCI Database
Qu Xia and Yang Xiaotong
Chinese Education & Society, volume 49, issue 1–2 (January 2016), pp. 99–113

For any permission-related enquiries please visit:
http://www.tandfonline.com/page/help/permissions

Notes on Contributors

Zhong Binglin is a professor at the Faculty of Education, Beijing Normal University, China, and president of the Chinese Society of Education.

Zhou Guangli is a professor at the Graduate School of Education, Renmin University of China.

Li Jiangbo is the deputy director of the Administrative Committee of Chengdu Economics & Technological Development Zone.

Zhang Junchao is an associate professor at the School of Education, Huazhong University of Science and Technology, China.

Chang Kai is the deputy director of the Graduate School of Fuzhou University, China.

Gong Le is the section chief of the Graduate School and assistant research fellow, Tianjin University, China.

Ding Ling is a member of staff at the Educational Administrative Office, Jianghan University, China.

Lin Mengquan is the deputy director of China Academic Degrees and Graduate Education Development Center in Beijing, China.

Wei Shuguang is an associate professor at the School of Education, Huazhong University of Science and Technology, China.

Liu Shuiyun is an associate professor in the Faculty of Education, Beijing Normal University, China.

Qiao Weifeng is an associate research fellow in the Institute of Education, Tsinghua University, China.

Qu Xia is an assistant professor at the China Institute of Industrial Relations, China.

Liu Xianjun is the deputy director of the Academic Council and professor at the School of Education, Huazhong University of Science and Technology, China.

Yang Xiaotong is a staff member at the Beijing Green Cultural Monuments Management Office, China.

Yu Yang is an associate professor at the Institute for Higher Education, Jilin University, China.

Zhang Yingqiang is dean and professor at the School of Education, Huazhong University of Science and Technology, China.

Su Yongjian is an assistant professor at the School of Higher Education, Dalian University of Technology, China.

Wang Yonglin is an associate research fellow at the Graduate School of Higher Education, Donghua University, China.

Wang Zhanjun is a professor at the Institute of Education, Beijing Institute of Technology, China, and a professor at the Institute of Education, Tsinghua University, China.

External Higher Education Quality Assurance System in China

Liu Shuiyun

In the midst of worldwide expansion of higher education, diversification of student populations, and diminished unit expenditure, quality assurance has become a central concern of higher education in many countries, while globalization of education market and university ranking all add fuel to the move of formulating quality frameworks within and beyond national boundaries.

Chinese higher education has gradually changed its elitist nature since its birth a century ago and embarked on an internationally recognized path of massification. There has been a dramatic expansion of enrollment in higher education since the end of the 1990s. China currently has the largest higher education system in the world. In 2014, it had 2,529 accredited universities and colleges, with a total student enrollment of 25.5 million. Accompanying the rapid growth of the higher education system, its quality has become a central focus in China over the last decade. Based on continuous policy design and reforms, an array of external quality assessment schemes of higher education has been established, which were operated by governments alongside the third-party evaluation agencies and the market.

State-run higher education assessment schemes were formulated in China at three levels in the following sequence: undergraduate education, postgraduate education, and vocational education and private higher education. Undergraduate level assessment was first to conducted in China. From 1994 to 2001, three forms of quality assessment, *quality accreditation, excellence assessment*, and *random assessment*, were put into practice in China. The Ministry of Education (MOE) combined the three quality assessment schemes together and launched a new project in 2002, the Quality Assessment of Undergraduate Education. According to this project, all higher education institutions providing undergraduate education should be compulsorily evaluated within a five-year period on a rolling basis. The evaluation is on the institutional level. The MOE established the Higher Education Evaluation Centre (HEEC) to conduct quality evaluation. The first round of reviews from 2002 to 2008 evaluated 589 higher education institutions. The second round of reviews started from the end of 2010, and mainly focuses on those higher education institutions with newly established undergraduate programs that have not been evaluated before.

Besides the HEEC, which undertakes the evaluation of undergraduate programs, another governmental quality assessment agency that focuses on postgraduate education was also founded, namely, the China Academic Degrees & Graduate Education Development Centre (CDGDC). It is engaged in the accreditation of postgraduate degree–granting units, the approval of national key disciplines of priority, as well as the review and selection of excellent master's and doctoral dissertations. Furthermore, the CDGDC initiated the Subject Evaluation program from 2002. The audit of vocational education and private institutions is conducted by the provincial accreditation committees. In 2008, the MOE launched the Project of Teaching Evaluation in Higher Vocational Education Institutions, which specified the evaluation procedures and indicators. The provinces are supposed to follow the project, design the detailed evaluation schemes, and operate the on-site evaluation. The MOE reserves the right to inspect the review processes of local governments.

Nongovernmental agencies have also engaged in higher education quality assessment in China since the 1990s, such as the Shanghai Agency for Education Evaluation and the Jiangsu Agency for Education Evaluation. They are qualified to undertake higher education quality assessment and accreditation with the delegation and assessment experts from the governments or the institutions. As governmental assessment agencies have engaged in almost all types of higher education evaluation, few opportunities have been left for these nongovernmental accreditation agencies to work alone or participate in any official evaluation schemes (Li 2004). Paralleling the formal quality assessment schemes, university rankings have also exercised considerable influence on the assessment of higher education institutions in China. They have been published since the end of the 1980s, mainly by for-profit educational companies, such as Netbig and the China University Alumni Association, while some research institutes also embraced the market. The rankings are very popular with the public, especially with the potential students and their parents.

To sum up, the developments of higher education in China over a quarter of a century have resulted in an array of external quality assurance schemes for higher education operated by governments, the third-party evaluation agencies and the market. Among them, the state is the leading actor and quality assessment is the dominant form. Yet, the higher education quality assessment mechanisms in China, which functioned over a decade, have both gained recognition and invited criticism. Some critics argued that the external quality assessment has not contributed to the improvement of quality in higher education. In this context, it is necessary to examine what measures have been implemented in China to ensure the higher education quality, and the extent to which these external quality assurance schemes have fulfilled the role of transforming the higher education institutions. It is expected that the experience drawn from the Chinese practices could be extended to other contexts, including Asian economies and the global South.

This issue includes eight journal articles published recently (2012–2015) from the top Chinese educational research journals, such as *Educational Research, Journal of Higher Education*, and *Fudan Education Forum*. Most of the authors are renowned educational researchers from higher education institutions funded by the "985 Project"[1] and the experts from the evaluation agencies of MOE. These papers cover different evaluation schemes, such as the quality evaluation of undergraduate education, postgraduate education evaluation, and vocational evaluation. A variety of research perspectives are adopted, including theoretical analysis, empirical study of the evaluation efficiency, and exploration of value orientations, and international comparison studies.

The first selected article is offered by Prof. Zhang Yingqiang, Dean of the School of Education, Huazhong University of Science of Technology and Su Yongjian, a doctoral student there. This article examines the quality assurance system from a theoretical perspective. They critically reflect the traditional higher education quality assurance system from three angles.

First, they regard higher education quality assurance as an ideology, and accountability is believed to be its key mission. The accountability schemes have eroded traditional professional autonomy and trust on higher education institutions. In this regard, higher education institutions gained legitimacy from external world but lost their own rationality. Second, they also see higher education quality assurance as a technology, which helps to measure and assess the quality of higher education. However, relying too much on quality assessment technology has made technology replace the purpose. Quality is then no longer regarded as a question of what it actually is, but something can be managed and measured. Third, they also take higher education quality assurance as a kind of power. Higher education institutions have to respond to various external requirements, which caused the academic tribes to be colonized. Based on the critical reflections on the traditional quality assurance schemes, Zhang and Su suggest that a holistic quality culture should be established. The new quality culture should be based on mutual trust among various stakeholders.

The second, third and fourth papers focus on a specific quality assessment scheme in China (i.e., the quality assessment of undergraduate education [QAUE]), one of the most influential state-run quality assessment schemes in China. The second paper is written by Liu Xianjun, Zhang Junchao, Wei Shuguang, and Ding Ling, professors from the School of Education, Huazhong University of Science of Technology, and Professor Yu Yang from Jilin University. They examine the effectiveness of the first-round of QAUE from 2003–2008. Based on a large-scale empirical study, the research group found that that QAUE has considerably pushed the evaluated institutions to improve their quality. For example, they have emphasized the role of undergraduate teaching, actively developed special characteristics of the institutions, improved their infrastructure, teaching facilities, and the quality of teaching staff, and also enhanced teaching management and internal quality assurance. QAUE has also caused some unexpected problems. For example, using the uniform evaluation criteria has led to the homogenization of higher education institutions, the role of provincial governments has been neglected, and the procedure of follow-up reforms has not been emphasized sufficiently. Based on the efficiency evaluation, the research team proposes some suggestions to improve the Chinese higher education quality assessment system.

The third paper by Professor Zhou Guangli from Renmin University of China. He takes QAUE as an example to examine the efficiency of Chinese higher education quality assurance system. The first round of the QAUE was recognized as being moderately effective, and left great room for improvement. According to the operational mechanism, the authors regard the QAUE as a state-run accountability system for higher education institutions. This is one kind of administrative accountability schemes led by the government, which is not believed to be effective in reality. Prof. Zhou also realizes that the external quality assessment purely organized by the nongovernment agencies is not possible in the current circumstances, because of the immature civil society in China. Thus, he suggests that China should move from the existing administrative accountability scheme to a social accountability scheme, where the involvements of both internal and external interest groups of higher education are encouraged. This scheme could be coordinated by the governments but organized by the governmental and nongovernmental agencies together. The social accountability scheme is believed to be able to fully mobilize the enthusiasm and initiatives of higher education stakeholders to participate in the supervision of colleges and universities. The author believes that this is the only way to enhance the effectiveness of Chinese higher education quality assessment system.

The fourth paper is written by Professor Zhong Binglin, the former president and an educational researcher from Beijing Normal University. He analyzed the Qualification Evaluation results of the newly established colleges (i.e., the second round of the QUAE) and described the development situation of Chinese undergraduate education programs with short history. The result analysis shows that the newly established colleges perform well in the dimensions of learning atmosphere construction and student training, and teaching quality. The evaluated colleges tend to be qualified in these two evaluation indicators. In contrast, most of the evaluated colleges are unqualified in the following evaluation indicators: the structure of teaching staff, university-industry collaboration education, specialty setup and structure adjustment, quality control, cultivation and training of teachers. In this regard, Zhong suggests that the newly established colleges in China should make efforts to optimize the structure of teaching staff. They also need to reform their mode of student training and to explore the methods of student training through university-industry collaboration. The newly established colleges should enhance the specialty construction and reforms, to meet the needs of economic and social development. In addition, the internal quality monitoring mechanisms in these newly established colleges should be improved to assure education quality. The feasible ways of teacher cultivation and training in the newly established colleges, especially in the private ones, should be further developed as well.

The fifth paper is offered by Dr. Wang Yonglin from Shanghai Jiao Tong University and Professor Wang Zhanjun from Beijing Institute of Technology. They concentrate on the vocational education evaluation. Based on the content analysis of two evaluation projects conducted in 2004 and 2008, they analyzed the value orientations of the quality evaluation of higher vocational education in China. They find that the higher vocational education evaluation in China intend to push the evaluated institutions to enhance quality awareness, establish their quality standards, emphasize the role of teaching, and highlight the characteristics of institutions. The value orientations have been altered from time to time to adapt to the changing external environments. They also indicate that the value orientations in Chinese higher vocational educational evaluation are not appropriate enough, as the evaluation started late and developed quite rapidly with less experience accumulation. Thus, they suggest that some of the value orientations should be further adjusted. For example, the implicit factors influencing educational quality should be emphasized; the participation of the evaluated institutions in the evaluation should be enhanced; the governance, management, and evaluation of higher vocational education should be separated; the quality monitoring should become normal, continuous, and dynamic.

The sixth paper focuses on the evaluation of postgraduate education, which is offered by Lin Mengquan from CDGDC, Chang Kai from Fuzhou University, and Gong Le from Tianjin University. They examine the higher education quality assurance systems in the United Kingdom, France, and the United States from an international comparison perspective, and draws the experiences for the quality evaluation of Chinese postgraduate education to learn. They find that the designs of higher education quality assurance systems in various national contexts are influenced by the higher education systems, traditional culture and social backgrounds there. The clearly defined and harmonious relationships of responsibility, rights and interests between various stakeholders in quality assurance are the pre-condition for the quality assurance mechanisms to effectively run in these countries. Furthermore, they also find that the model combining both internal and external quality assurance, while giving priority to the self-evaluation of higher education institutions is the future tendency of higher education quality assurance development. In the context of higher education globalization and internationalization, the quality assurance mechanisms also tend to be internationalized. Referring to the experiences learning from the quality assurance systems in the three countries, the authors propose some suggestions for improving the Chinese quality assurance of postgraduate education.

The seventh paper is offered by Professor Wang Zhanjun from Beijing Institute of Technology and two doctoral students from Tsinghua University, Qiao Weifeng and Li Jiangbo. They introduce a new higher education quality assessment technology, monitoring evaluation. Higher education monitoring evaluation is defined as a process that uses modern information technology to continually collect and deeply analyze relevant data, visually present the status of higher education, and provide objective basis for value judgments and scientific decision making. The authors emphasize that monitoring evaluation is a data-intensive evaluation. The temporal scale is intensive, the spatial scale is diverse, and the value scale is multiple. The usage of monitoring aims to provide promote feedback for continuous quality improvement, to follow the systematic change of higher education for scientific decision-making, to deliver user-oriented information service for diverse value judgments. The technology of higher education monitoring evaluation includes data collection and consolidation, data mining and analysis, and data visualization. The authors believe that the emergence of monitoring evaluation is a result of rapid development of information technology, which meets the needs of higher education system changes and governance adjustments. Monitoring evaluation was also initiated in China. HEEC has established the database of basic status of undergraduate education, to provide support for the second-round of QAUE.

The last paper is by Dr. Qu Xia and Yang Xiaotong from Renmin University. The authors describe the research situation of Chinese higher education quality in the last 15 years. A total of 1,048 academic papers about higher education quality selected from a key Chinese social science research database (CSSCI) are analyzed. A keyword co-occurrence knowledge mapping is made by using CiteSpace and the main research topics and their evolution tendency in this field are outlined. The further analysis shows that Chinese higher education quality research is highly influenced by the national education reform policies, and there is a good interaction between research and policy. The release of national educational policies would stimulate the emergence of new research topics, and the academic discussions about the educational reforms will further facilitate the improvement of the related policies. Apart from the policy discussions of higher education quality, the main research topics include quality views of mass higher education, teaching management of higher education institutions, student cultivation, and higher education quality assurance and evaluation. The issue of quality assurance and evaluation is always the research focus in this field. The issues of teaching management and student cultivation have emerged recently and might become the future hot topics. However, the related research tends to be superficial, and thus deeper and more feasible research about these topics is particularly needed in China.

These eight articles are the most representative research findings about Chinese higher education quality assurance, published recently. The various evaluation schemes are discussed, including quality assessment of undergraduate education, quality evaluation of higher vocational education and quality assurance of postgraduate education. They discussed the achievements these evaluation schemes have gained, and the problems and challenges they have to face. The existing quality assurance mechanisms are reflected, based on theoretical analysis and empirical studies. The international experience is referred. Some suggestions are also proposed to improve the current mechanisms, including establishing new quality culture, shifting the value orientation behind the quality assessment designs, adopting social accountability schemes to replace the administrative ones, using the new evaluation technology such as monitoring evaluation, and establishing a combination model of internal and external quality assurance schemes. On the whole, the analysis of the existing evaluation schemes and the suggestions for the future development made in the eight papers shows a changing trend in the field of Chinese higher education quality assurance from emphasizing quality evaluation to concerning about quality improvement. Although establishing a better quality assurance system is always a research focus of this field, as found by Qu and Yang in the last paper, nowadays researchers paid more attention to essential quality improvement, especially the improvement of student learning outcomes, through various evaluation and assurance mechanisms. This is also an international trend, which has been emphasized by scholars before (Harvey and Newton 2004; Eaton 2012). The quality assurance schemes in western countries, such as the United Kingdom and the United States, also follow this trend and identify the improvement of student learning outcomes as their main objective of external quality assurance, as indicated by Lin et al. in the sixth paper of this issue. It is expected that the future quality assurance schemes of Chinese higher education might also concentrate their efforts on quality improvement.

FUNDING

This paper is supported by the Fundamental Research Funds for the Central Universities (SKZZX2013021).

NOTE

1. The 985 Project began in 1998 and has sponsored 39 Chinese universities to build "world-class" universities with advanced research outcomes and a high international reputation.

REFERENCES

Eaton, J. S. 2012. The future of accreditation? *Planning for Higher Education* 40 (3):8–15.

Harvey, L., and J. Newton. 2004. Transforming quality evaluation. *Quality in Higher Education* 10 :149–65. doi:10.1080/1353832042000230635

Li, Y. 2004. Revision and introspection of the construction of higher education assessment system in China. *Journal of Jiangsu Institute of Education (Social Science)* 20 (2): 24–46. (in Chinese).

Quality Assurance in Higher Education: Reflection, Criticism, and Change

Zhang Yingqiang and Su Yongjian

Abstract: Quality assurance in modern higher education is both an accountability-oriented ideology and a technological method. It has also evolved into a increasingly rationalist and professionalized power mechanism. Its advocacy of compliance, technological mythology, and imbalance between power and responsibility are inherent disadvantages of higher education quality assurance at present. To sustainably improve higher education quality, the current concern must change from quality assurance to quality culture. We should reflect on and innovate the traditional quality assurance in higher education. At the same time, it is necessary to build a holistic quality culture among various stakeholders based on mutual trust and a social contract.

There have been quality problems in higher education for some time but, during most of their histories, quality problems at colleges and universities have been addressed by their faculty members, either individually or collectively (Jones 2013). Higher education continually expanded in the twentieth century (Schofer and Meyer 2005) and colleges and universities became increasingly rationalized (Ramirez 2006). Since the 1980s, the question of quality, originally considered embedded in the internal work of higher education institutions, moved beyond institutional boundaries and evolved into a social and political issue involving multiple stakeholders. To respond to diverse stakeholder concerns about the quality in higher education, "countries around the world established and improved quality assurance systems for higher education with the hope of improving the quality of higher education in their countries or regions" (Su 2013). In terms of actual effects, however, such a rationalized quality assurance system has not operated as expected in practice (Tight 2003). After years of exploration and research, people have gradually come to realize that higher education quality assurance is not a myth, but rather a socially constructed reality. In other words, while the traditional discourse and practice of quality assurance has aided higher education institutions in addressing quality problems, it has gradually become enveloped in a rationalist "cage," leading to various

English translation © 2016 Taylor & Francis, Inc., from the Chinese text "Gaodeng jiaoyu zhiliang baozhang: Fansi, pipan yu biange" by Zhang Yingqiang and Su Yongjian. Translated by Michelle LeSourd. Originally published in *Jiaoyu yanjiu* [Educational Research], 2014, vol. 5.

irrational consequences. To continuously improve the quality of higher education, we must therefore re-examine the theory and practice of quality assurance, and on this basis find new possibilities for quality improvement.

In this article, we attempt to critically interpret higher education quality assurance in terms of three meanings or levels, and seek a path to quality assurance that moves beyond the traditional shortcomings. Taking into account the unique characteristics of academia and the different quality demands of multiple stakeholders, we believe that creating a holistic quality culture encompassing the whole society is the best choice to fundamentally improve the quality of higher education.

HIGHER EDUCATION QUALITY ASSURANCE AS AN IDEOLOGY

The economic downturn of the late 1970s led to unsustainable welfare policies in Western countries, and how to best provide public welfare became a key feature of policy agendas (Salter and Tapper 2000). Against this backdrop, the public sector, including higher education, saw the introduction of the neoliberal concepts of "economy," "efficiency," and "effectiveness," as well as the new public management movement's policy techniques of "decentralization," "marketization," "managerialism," and "performance," which originated in the private sectors (Ball 2003). These were meant to change a widely disparaged situation characterized by "bureaucracy," "centralization," "inefficiency," and a "decline in quality." In the field of higher education, national and regional quality assurance entities were established and adopted numerous measures to supervise and control the quality at colleges and universities.

In modern society, the emergence of higher education quality assurance indicated that university autonomy no longer existed in the traditional sense, and that governments and society no longer trusted higher education institutions. By controlling funding sources and choices, they forced higher education to report, explain, prove, and respond to the outside world about the efficiency and effectiveness of their resource use (Trow 1996). This loss of trust and the increasing demands of external stakeholders signaled a new era of accountability for higher education. The key new managerialist concepts of market competition, efficiency, effectiveness, and added value continually flooded into the traditional higher education system. Studies have shown that, even in the United Kingdom with its long tradition of university autonomy, managerialism has permeated the universities as a universal ideology (Deem and Brehony 2005). Accountability and new managerialism provide the theoretical explanation and support for governments and society to intervene in higher education. In practice, as a primary vehicle for accountability, higher education quality assurance absorbed these concepts, once commonly seen as private sector values, and made them more specific. As quality assurance developed further, such concepts permeated all levels of the quality assurance system, and became the guiding ideology for quality assurance in higher education. This ideology is typically reflected in accountability, supervision, control, performance, and value for money. In this sense, higher education quality assurance itself has evolved into an ideology occupying a hegemonic position. Its appearance as an ideology was an "epistemological revolution" in the history of higher education. Since then, the question of how to define and judge quality is no longer just the internal affair of higher education institutions; numerous stakeholders, including governments, society, and companies, have the right to express their views and demands concerning the quality of higher education. This suggests that unified higher education quality standards based on the common concepts of an elite community of scholars (Zhao 2008) are being replaced by pluralistic quality standards based on the diverse needs of society.

As an ideology, higher education quality assurance has an all-encompassing range, presents itself in flexible ways, and is capable of legitimizing ambitious alliances between existing and emerging groups in higher education politics (Salter and Tapper 2000). In a positive sense, higher education quality assurance as an ideology seeks to assist higher education institutions facing today's uncertain environment by means of multiparty participation and dialogue. Traditional professional and personal accountability has therefore gradually declined, while accountability to market forces and government has grown. As an ideology, higher education quality assurance commingles the interrelated but conflicting value demands and discourse systems of governments, markets, society, business, students, and other stakeholders. Higher education quality assurance is an expression of the government's pragmatic philosophy for colleges and universities to produce more high-level scientific research and talent to serve the national interests. It also embodies the utilitarian value of efficiency above all else: that markets demand the effective use of resources by institutions of higher education. Quality assurance in higher education has also begun to include student learning outcomes assessments in recent years, reflecting a student-centered educational philosophy. Since the 1980s, the most notable change in the transformation of American higher education accreditation organizations has been an increase in student assessments, indicating a shift in emphasis from resources invested to the student learning process (Guo and Shi 2012). Currently, student learning outcomes have become the basis and focus of judging the quality of institutions under higher education accreditation (Brittingham 2009). Even more positive is that advances in higher education quality assurance have also aided many colleges and universities in developing a quality culture (Danø and Stensaker 2007). As some researchers have pointed out, the data and reports in *Examining Quality Culture in Higher Education Institutions*, a survey conducted by the European University Association (EUA), suggest that "the majority of surveyed European institutions have created a preliminary awareness of quality culture" (Wen 2012).

Consequently, many national and regional governments, institutions, and professional bodies are actively committed to quality assurance in higher education. It appears as though institutions of higher education can use quality assurance to effectively deal with all of the difficulties and challenges in modern society. As an ideology, however, the external control, efficiency orientation, standardization, and unification of higher education quality assurance tends to erode autonomy, equity, diversity, and other traditional values of academic organizations (Su 2013), thereby threatening the sustainable development of higher education. After examining the issues of trust, control, professional autonomy, and accountability in higher education quality assurance in the United Kingdom, Andreas Hoecht said that accountability and transparency are important principles in which academic personnel should wholeheartedly believe. Nevertheless, quality assurance based on audits and controls to some extent weakens the professional autonomy and trust of such personnel, has a high opportunity cost, and is not conducive to innovative teaching (Hoecht 2006). In the long run, as an ideology, the rationalist and instrumentalist characteristics of higher education quality assurance easily lead to a form of discourse hegemony with the result that, as quality assurance helps institutions to build a quality culture, it may also create a compliance culture, thereby inhibiting creativity and ultimately deviating from the goals of higher education quality assurance itself.

As an ideology, higher education quality assurance is a double-edged sword. On one hand, it enables higher education to respond effectively to the challenges brought by massification, markets, and internationalization, thereby protecting the legitimacy of higher education in modern society. On the other hand, control, efficiency, performance, and other values, with accountability at the core, have become the new management philosophy at some institutions. These have constantly eroded traditional professional autonomy and trust, with the result that higher education is regaining its legitimacy in modern society while losing its rationality.

HIGHER EDUCATION QUALITY ASSURANCE AS A TECHNOLOGY

Throughout the history of higher education, examinations, vocational qualification certification systems, and peer reviews were the primary means of quality control among traditional colleges and universities. The origins of modern higher education quality assurance can be traced back to higher education accreditation in the United States during the late nineteenth and early twentieth centuries (Zhang 2005). Today, accreditation remains a primary form of higher education quality assurance in some countries and regions, particularly in North America and Central, Northern, and Eastern Europe. Later, university rankings, graduate tracking, and other surveys by governments and professional bodies entered the higher education domain, laying the foundation for the modern, large-scale, and organized higher education quality assurance system. The "systematic and formal" higher education quality assurance we are discussing today arose only in the 1980s and 1990s, however, which followed state policy intervention in higher education, the broad application of assessments, the further development of accreditation and ranking, and the impact of business and industry quality assurance methods such as benchmarking and performance indicators (Anderson 2006).

If higher education quality assurance as an ideology has influenced the development of modern higher education in terms of ideas and values, then the related policies, assessments, audits, accreditation, ranking, benchmarking, and performance indicators become the intermediary methodologies of higher education quality assurance ideology. We can refer to them as higher education quality assurance technology. In this sense, higher education quality assurance, as we refer to it today, is a collective term for all of the techniques and methods developed as higher education has evolved.

In May 1991, the United Kingdom issued a white paper, *Higher Education: A New Framework,* which clearly listed quality control, quality audits, and quality assessment as the three major higher education quality assurance mechanisms. The European Association for Quality Assurance in Higher Education surveyed its member organizations. It found that assessment, auditing, accreditation, and benchmarking were four ways in which European institutions often conducted quality reviews (Zhao 2008).

Quality assessment has been the most commonly used mechanism among these specific higher education quality assurance methods. "Beginning with the global quality assurance movement in the 1980s, quality assessment has been the primary technology of quality assurance" (Yang et al. 2013). The shadow of quality assessment can be seen in any higher education quality assurance system; China's undergraduate education quality assurance system is an example of using assessment as the primary technological method. Today, assessment as a quality assurance technology has been widely applied to all levels of the quality assurance system. For example, the direct assessment of student learning outcomes has become the primary means of supporting institutional decision-making and increasing quality in many countries, including the United States, the United Kingdom, Australia, and Japan.

Measurement is the basis and premise of assessment (Xu 2012). To assess the learning outcomes and experiences of college students, many countries such as the United States have developed a wide variety of tools for measuring quality. With these relatively scientific measurement tools and techniques, we are able to turn "quality," a concept that people often think is difficult to measure, into an operable practical process, and then adopt appropriate policies and measures to improve the daily practice of teaching and management of an institution. Among these measurement tools, the most influential ones are the National Survey of Student Engagement, the College Student Experiences Questionnaire, and the University of California Undergraduate Experience Survey in the United States, as well as the UK's National Student Survey. Since the establishment of a student-centered philosophy in the higher education domain and the deepening of globalization in higher education, these survey tools have crossed international borders to be emulated by other countries and regions. At the same time, the Organizatino for Economic Cooperation and Development and other international organizations are actively promoting assessment activities and practices related to student learning outcomes. Peter Ewell (2008) reminds us that, despite significant progress in assessment technology, we cannot rely on one method to solve all problems. In addition to assessments, other quality assurance systems widely used in modern higher education include audits, performance indicators, and benchmarking. For example, the UK's Higher Education Quality Assurance Agency, in response to institutions' doubts about assessment, combined discipline and institutional evaluations into an institutional audit that did not directly assess quality, but rather focused on improving the internal quality assurance systems of the audited institutions. Similarly, China is primarily using audit assessment rather than direct assessment in its new round of undergraduate teaching assessment. In addition, "within a QA framework, quality is treated as a synonym for 'performance.' Its advocates require the imposition of technical instruments, such as performance indicators to measure the input and output of educational spending and resources. This instrumental view of quality validates the use of quantitative measures such as the numbers of graduates, the number of post-graduate students, research income and so on as indicators of performance" (Sachs 1994). In a sense, without these quantitative performance indicators, quality accountability would not make sense. Of course, what we must do is to use judgment to reconcile these statistics (Elton 1988).

"From a technical perspective, quality initiatives are often reduced to series of steps with clearly identifiable actors and predictable outcomes" (Ramirez 2013). The key feature of higher education quality assurance as a technology is therefore to view quality as something existing objectively that can be broken down and measured. Such an "instrumental practice" attempts to improve measurement tools and indicators to allow us to intervene in the higher education quality agenda and everyday practice, thereby achieving the purpose of accountability or increased quality. In today's extremely complex and uncertain times, quality assurance as a technology has a very important practical significance. It allows us to control the quality of higher education to a certain extent but, more importantly, it allows multiple stakeholders to perceive the certainty of higher education quality, thereby maintaining the legitimate status of higher education in modern society. But we must note here that quality assurance technology does not produce quality on its own. Realities tell us again and again that quality assurance as a technological

11

method does not automatically translate into action and practice to improve the quality of higher education; "good technology may also mean bad teaching" (Young 2004).

In short, while quality assurance as a technological method helps us to measure and assess the quality of higher education, it also dismembers or reduces what was once a full and meaningful quality to a purely technical or quantitative concept (Engebretsen, Heggen, and Eilertsen 2012). Quality is then "no longer regarded as a question of what it actually is, but as a question of how to manage and measure it" (Wang and Lu 2013). Even more seriously, under the dominance of technological rationalism, the myth surrounding the various technological methods of quality assurance results in an everyday practice with "technology as its purpose." The technology begins exceed its own boundaries and take on a connotation of power.

HIGHER EDUCATION QUALITY ASSURANCE AS POWER

Quality assurance in higher education, in the modern sense, originated mainly in business and industry, which are intrinsically different from academic organizations. Driven by multiple stakeholders, higher education quality assurance has become, since its earliest emergence, a complex mixture of ideology, power relations, and interest considerations. Through both theoretical examination and observation of the everyday practices of institutions, we therefore find that higher education quality assurance is no longer purely a technological method used to protect or enhance quality; in its own right, it is highly correlated with power (Barnett 1994). To some extent, it has even evolved into a power mechanism, with accountability as the core ideology, that reflects the positional relationships of different interest groups. John Brennan believes that "the debate about the quality assessment of the higher education system and the quality assessment of institutions is a debate centering around power" (Brennan 2005). In addition, as part of the continual power struggle for control of high-status knowledge, quality assurance brings together technology, bureaucracy, and value elements by granting power to certain groups while depriving others of power (Salter and Tapper 2000).

During the step-by-step process of rationalization, higher education quality assurance as a kind of power gradually alters the power divisions within and outside institutions. The appearance of quality assurance indicates that the power to define and assess quality is increasingly transferred into the hands of external stakeholders. Such a transfer of power breaks the power monopoly of academic personnel to define and practice quality, enabling more stakeholders to intervene in the quality assurance agenda, so that traditional academic work continues to reflect the interests and demands of the external community. Meanwhile, inside colleges and universities, power is concentrated in administrative personnel, which makes institutions more flexible in handling daily affairs, and they become more progressive organizations. The re-division of power therefore provides a realistic possibility for institutions to change and update themselves for today's society.

Nevertheless, quality assurance as power is itself full of paradoxes. With regard to the relationships between universities, government, society, and markets, during the process of reconstructing these power relationships the government, as the primary controller of higher education resources, uses quality assurance methods and findings to allocate relatively scarce financial resources. In order to win the competition for funding and resources, many institutions compromise with the government by turning over some of their power and accepting the government's quality standards and objectives. Such a power spillover occurs not only in higher education systems moving from decentralization toward centralization, but also in systems that are transitioning in the opposite direction. In the power genealogy of modern higher education quality assurance, although government power was once weakened or resisted, due to the importance of quality higher education to global competition and the high dependence of higher education institutions on external resources, the government is bound to intervene in the quality assurance agenda by using performance indicators and related quality policies as leverage for resource allocation. Of course, this power relationship is not explicitly and nakedly controlling and being controlled, but is expressed as an implicit and undeclared "technical discipline." The government will not directly intervene too much in the internal daily management of institutions, but rather will achieve the supervision and monitoring of quality in higher education institutions by developing complex and demanding performance indicators and rigorous, high-stakes assessments (Li et al. 2012). In some respects, exerting the pressure of external control mechanisms to ensure higher education quality is a reflection of the increasingly tense relationships between the state and higher education institutions (Filippakou and Tapper 2010). In addition, the power relationships between institutions, markets, and society are also shifting under the impact of the higher education quality assurance movement. The discourse about quality standards and the manner in which to carry out quality assurance is being shared and even expropriated by markets and society. The "Darwinism," consumer choice, and public evaluation and opinion of market competition have become important parameters for judging the quality of higher education. Looking at college and university rankings as a quality assurance mechanism, the debate over their strengths and weaknesses has repeatedly demonstrated that such rankings have become a power mechanism affecting how institutions define quality and determine the direction of their own development.

While affecting the power relationships between institutions and external stakeholders, the rationalization and professionalization of quality assurance are also constantly changing the power distribution within higher education institutions (Brennan and Shah 2000). To cater to the different quality demands of external stakeholders and to diverse assessment standards, institutional management "empowers" academic professionals with greater autonomy to enable them to "freely" adjust the focus and content of their academic work. Meanwhile, the institutions to some extent refine the external stakeholders' utilitarian definition of quality into criteria for appraising academic personnel, supported by incentive systems to induce and compel them to comply. In the process of formulating such quality policies and practicing quality assurance procedures, the discretion of managers inside the institutions continues to increase, while the professional authority of academic personnel becomes more restricted, turning them into "managed professionals" (Zhang 2012).

This phenomenon is particularly evident in countries and regions in which neoliberal philosophy and its related technologies attempt to ensure and improve the quality of higher education. An observation and study of academic professions in the United Kingdom showed that, throughout the academic year, all academic personnel at all universities not only had to organize their teaching according to the indicator system of the teaching quality assessment, but also had to participate in a fiercely competitive and high-stakes scientific research assessment. Academic personnel who have always favored freedom and enjoyed great autonomy must constantly deal with external and internal reviews. In such a situation, teaching freedom is thoroughly destroyed, and the free space for research is also severely compressed

(Huang 2013). On the surface, under modern higher education quality assurance, academics can rely on the autonomy of their specialty to protect traditional "academic tribe." In fact, however, under the power genealogy of quality assurance, the autonomy of academic personnel has been sidelined into the hands of others. They must not only accept monitoring and appraisal by external stakeholders, but must also "please" the administrative personnel and students who have an important influence on the advancement and development of their academic careers.

When higher education quality assurance as power places academic occupational groups under the control of administrative power, it creates a split within the academic profession. In the practice of higher education quality assurance, it is common for academic personnel who internalize the external quality assurance requirements and put them into academic practice to receive a variety of incentives and accolades, and also to imperceptibly take control of the academic discourse about quality. The "symbols" and "discourse" that quality assurance grants to certain groups are essentially embodied in a power relationship. Academic personnel who can "win" on quality assurance no doubt have greater power than the "losers." Vigilance is warranted because quality assurance results in the bestowing and transfer of power, and the implied "rules of the game" of quality assurance tend to produce an interactive magnifying effect. Academic quality is therefore constantly being shaped by the power of quality assurance, and academia has increasingly become an arena rife with power struggles.

In short, by conferring more power upon stakeholders, higher education quality assurance as power can flexibly reflect external demands, while also causing the "colonization" of academic tribes. In this situation, academic personnel frequently cater to quality assurance on the surface, but secretly resist or dispel it (Anderson 2006). Ironically, even as their substantive powers continue to decline, academic personnel are asked to assume more and more responsibility for quality assurance.

REBUILDING TRUST AND DEVELOPING A HIGHER EDUCATION QUALITY CULTURE

In this article, our interpretation of three dimensions of higher education quality assurance is intended to reveal the complexity of quality assurance and the inherent paradox of the values and implications that it conveys. On the actual higher education quality agenda, there are no clear boundaries between quality assurance as an ideology, as a technology, and as power. The three are mutually intertwined and collectively impact higher education practice.

The paradox exhibited by traditional higher education quality assurance is rooted in the unidirectional accountability of its ideology. In such a unidirectional paradigm of accountability, higher education quality is narrowly defined to satisfy the requirements of external stakeholders. Under the guidance of positivist ideas, this extremely utilitarian definition is then built into an indicator system that can, through a variety of techniques, be broken down, measured, and turned into a ranking system. Those intrinsic aspects of quality that are difficult to turn into indicators, but have educational significance, are disregarded or even hidden from view. In addition, to constantly adapt to the centrality of external demand, the increasingly technological quality assurance also continues to shrink the boundaries of the academic community's quality discourse and activities. The extension and penetration of external power into the academic community causes it to transform into an agent that executes external quality standards and rules rather than acting as a quality assurance body. In a word, under the traditional paradigm of quality assurance in higher education, a rigorous external accountability replaces mutual trust between stakeholders. Ironically, however, the more stringent and specific the accountability, the fewer the facts it is able to reveal (Trow 1996). It is therefore difficult for a simple technological improvement to fundamentally break through the paradox of higher education quality assurance, and change is imperative.

The only long-term solution to fundamentally improve the quality of higher education and move beyond traditional quality assurance is a quality culture that fosters communication, exchange, and dialogue throughout the whole society, based on a "new social contract of mutual trust" (Kehm 2012). This new quality culture encompasses not only an internal institutional culture centered on improving quality, but also the responsibility of the academic community to external stakeholders, and public trust in higher education (Kennedy 2002).

First, we must treat higher education institutions well, appreciate and cherish their autonomy and academic freedom, and create throughout society a "social and cultural consensus" of respect for the academic freedom and autonomy of colleges and universities (Zhang and Jiang 2013); to this end we must normalize the actions of the various stakeholders. Higher education quality assurance practices characterized by accountability have fully demonstrated that the quality terminology and tools arising out of industry and commerce are not fully applicable to higher education (Houston 2008). Such quality assurance imposed upon institutions from the outside, characterized by bureaucracy and "proceduralism," not only destroys the trust between external stakeholders and the academic community, but also undermines the collegial spirit and reduces university faculty members' sense of moral responsibility (Gosling and D'Andrea 2001). Moreover, as the development of quality assurance deepens, the academic community in turn no longer trusts external quality assurance that claims "to help colleges and universities improve quality." To fundamentally improve the quality of higher education, we must therefore fully consider the organizational characteristics of institutions and the specialized character of academic work. In such a highly specialized field, the academic community's definition of quality will naturally be different than that of its external stakeholders. Within the academic community there has always been a tradition of internal control of teaching and research. Stakeholders are at a great distance from these processes, lack professional expertise and capacity, and therefore have difficulty controlling the internal affairs of academic institutions (Huisman and Currie 2004). To enable institutions to continue meeting the needs of external stakeholders, we must establish a new kind of contractual relationship based on trust between the institutions and the stakeholders. A fundamental principle is to create consensus and action throughout society to respect and protect academic freedom and the autonomy of higher education institutions. History tells us that, without autonomy and academic freedom, academic institutions have a slim chance of maintaining diversity and vitality of knowledge and responding to societal needs and changes (Zumeta 1998).

In addition, power and responsibility are not equal in the quality assurance process. In particular, as the power of academic personnel is declining while their responsibility is increasing, it is necessary to promote the shared responsibility of all stakeholders throughout society, to fundamentally improve the quality of higher education and avoid quality "becoming an unspecified consumer demand, or simply becoming a tool for national competition" (Shen and Lu 2011). In modern society, all responsibility relationships are mutually beneficial; "if the official authorities make subordinates accountable for certain actions or outcomes, then the authorities have an equal and complementary responsibility to ensure that the subordinates have the capacity to complete the tasks and to give them enough support" (Lu and Wang 2013). Under this paradigm of shared responsibility, higher education quality assurance can become "public space" for the free discussion of quality issues, rather than simply a link in a linear chain conveying external quality demands. In such a public space, the various stakeholders can engage in a full dialogue and negotiations about the concepts, procedures, techniques, methods, and consequences of the higher education quality agenda, avoiding dominant interest groups exerting unidirectional control over academic quality and thereby hampering academic innovation and student development. Related empirical studies also show that higher education faculty involvement in the quality assessment process significantly reduces the likelihood of their believing that quality assurance involves instrumental rationality (Trullen and Rodriguez 2013). If higher education quality assurance cannot win the support of academic groups, it is unlikely to serve the development of higher education. Emphasizing compliance with and being accountable to quality assurance will lead to the danger of isolating academic personnel and will jeopardize the entire institutional culture of the higher education system (Hodson and Thomas 2003). Future higher education quality assurance must also pay more attention to the importance and value of student participation (Coates 2005).

Finally, creating an internal quality culture that facilitates an institution's organizational innovation can also promote the development of individuals (academic personnel and students). In such a quality culture, academic personnel and students are the main quality bodies. The definition of quality is no longer to continually satisfy the demands of external stakeholders, but rather to fully account for the specialized nature of academic work and the natural laws of student development, and to adapt to social demands in an autonomous and constructive manner. European quality culture projects emphasize that quality cannot be defined in a top-down manner but should be defined by each institution, because applying a shared definition of quality to institutions with different missions and objectives is not feasible, and even disappointing (European University Association 2014). Improving quality by means of the people involved in an institution's internal quality culture greatly expands the scope of traditional quality assurance. A quality culture encourages each institution to define quality based on its own history, mission, goals, location, and environment, and to use a quality culture awareness to organically bring together multiple internal stakeholders, including administrators, faculty, and students, to work together to improve quality through negotiation and dialogue. Such a quality culture uses a "contextual" approach to integrate the concept of quality's self-improvement into the everyday management of the institution, the academic practices of the faculty, and the learning process of students; it breaks free of the traditional higher education quality assurance paradigm of "decontextualization" and the widely decried crisis of autonomy and academic freedom triggered by external accountability. Of course, a quality culture is not formed automatically; it requires highly proficient management and leadership. We must bear in mind, however, that a quality culture is not created just because the leadership proclaims it; it comes about through constantly learning the meaning of quality and its significance to practice, and through embedding "quality thinking" into practice (Yorke 2000).

The previous reflections, criticism, and corrections regarding higher education quality assurance do not constitute its wholesale negation. Protecting institutional autonomy, continuing academic freedom, sharing responsibility, and even creating a new quality culture are all inseparable from specific quality assurance processes and technological methods. Nor can we rule out the participation of and accountability to various stakeholders. Even the quality culture projects in Europe, which have attracted widespread attention and praise, fully account for the rationality of the existing higher education quality assurance system. The European University Association believes that any quality culture is based on two distinct components. The first is a set of values, beliefs, expectations, and commitments aimed at quality (the psychological aspect, referring to understanding, flexibility, participation, hopes, and emotions). The second component is about structural or managerial, and it includes a clear process for improving quality and coordinating all aspects (referring to the tasks, standards, and responsibilities of individuals, entities, and services; Harvey and Stensaker 2008; European University Association 2014).

In short, to fundamentally improve the quality of higher education, we need to extend beyond the traditional paradigm of higher education quality assurance and move toward quality culture. We must continually reaffirm the new quality culture in the broadest sense: it is a holistic quality culture philosophy that includes institutional quality culture, is based on a new trust, and encompasses the whole society. This holistic concept of quality culture does not simply revert to institutional traditions, but constitutes an upgrade and evolution that take the institutional mission to a higher level.

REFERENCES

Anderson, G. 2006. Assuring quality/resisting quality assurance: Academics' responses to 'quality' in some Australian universities. *Quality in Higher Education* 12:161–73. doi:10.1080/13538320600916767

Ball, S. J. 2003. The teacher's soul and the terrors of performativity. *Journal of Education Policy* 18:215–28. doi:10.1080/0268093022000043065

Barnett, R. 1994. Power, enlightenment and quality evaluation. *European Journal of Education* 29:165. doi:10.2307/1561639

Brennan, J. 2005. Higher education assessment in Europe. In *The state, higher education, and markets*, ed. M. Henkel and B. Little. Chinese ed., 221. Beijing: Educational Science Publishing House.

Brennan, J., and T. Shah. 2000. Quality assessment and institutional change: Experiences from 14 countries. *Higher Education* 3.

Brittingham, B. 2009. Accreditation in the United States: How did we get to where we are? *New Directions for Higher Education* 2009:7–27. doi:10.1002/he.331

Coates, H. 2005. The value of student engagement for higher education quality assurance. *Quality in Higher Education* 11:25–36. doi:10.1080/13538320500074915

Danø, T., and B. Stensaker. 2007. Still balancing improvement and accountability? Developments in external quality assurance in the Nordic countries 1996–2006. *Quality in Higher Education* 13:81–93. doi:10.1080/13538320701272839

Deem, R., and K. Brehony. 2005. Management as ideology: The case of 'new managerialism' in higher education. *Oxford Review of Education* 31:217–35. doi:10.1080/03054980500117827

Elton, L. 1988. Accountability in higher education: The danger of unintended consequences. *Higher Education* 17:377–90. doi:10.1007/bf00139535

Engebretsen, E., K. Heggen, and H. A. Eilertsen. 2012. Accreditation and power: A discourse analysis of a new regime of governance in higher education. *Scandinavian Journal of Educational Research* 56:401–17. doi:10.1080/00313831.2011.599419

European University. 2014. Quality culture in European universities: A bottom-up approach. http://www.eua.be/eua/jsp/en/upload/Quality_Culture_2002_2003.1150459570109 Accessed on 2014–01–24.

Ewell, P. T. 2008. Assessment and accountability in America today: Background and context. In Assessing and accounting for student learning: Beyond the spellings commission. *New Directions for Institutional Research (Special Issue Supplement)*, 7–17, 83–89.

Filippakou, O., and T. Tapper. 2010. The state and the quality agenda: A theoretical approach. *Higher Education Policy* 23:475–91. doi:10.1057/hep.2010.19

Gosling, D., and V. D'Andrea. 2001. Quality development: A new concept for higher education. *Quality in Higher Education* 7:7–17. doi:10.1080/13538320120045049

Guo, F. F., and J. H. Shi. 2012. Quyu renzheng zhong de xuesheng pingjia: 'Fengzi chenghun' yihuo 'tian zuo zhi he'?–Meiguo gaodeng jiaoyu zhiliang baozhang jizhi yanjiu [Student assessment in regional certification: "shotgun marriage" or "match made in heaven"?–The U.S. Higher education quality assurance mechanism]. *Waiguo jiaoyu yanjiu [Studies in Foreign Education]* 10.

Harvey, L., and B. Stensaker. 2008. Quality culture: Understandings, boundaries and linkages. *European Journal of Education* 43:427–42. doi:10.1111/j.1465–3435.2008.00367.x

Hodson, P., and H. Thomas. 2003. Quality assurance in higher education: Fit for the new millennium or simply year 2000 compliant? *Higher Education* 3.

Hoecht, A. 2006. Quality assurance in UK higher education: Issues of trust, control, professional autonomy and accountability. *Higher Education* 51:541–63. doi:10.1007/s10734-004-2533-2

Houston, D. 2008. Rethinking quality and improvement in higher education. *Quality Assurance in Education* 16:61–79. doi:10.1108/09684880810848413

Huang, Y. T. 2013. Xin gonggong guanli gaige zhong de Yingguo xueshu zhiye biange [UK academic occupational changes amidst new public management reform]. *Gaodeng jiaoyu yanjiu [Journal of Higher Education Research]* 5.

Huisman, J., and J. Currie. 2004. Accountability in higher education: Bridge over troubled water? *Higher Education* 48:529–51. doi:10.1023/b:high.0000046725.16936.4c

Jones, G. A. 2013. Governing quality: Positioning student learning as a core objective of institutional and system-level governance. In Keynote paper presented at the International Conference on Higher Education Student Learning and Development in a Globalizing Time. Hosted by the Institute of Education, Tsinghua University, Beijing, China: 27–28.

Kehm, B. 2012. Daxue paiming dui Ouzhou gaodeng jiaoyu tixi de yingxiang [The impacts of rankings on the european higher education landscape]. *As translated and reprinted in Beijing daxue jiaoyu pinglun [Peking University Education Review]* 3.

Kennedy, D. 2002. *Academic duty*. Cambridge, MA: Harvard University Press.

Li, L. L., N. G. Lu, and W. H. Li. 2012. "Xin gonggong guanli gainian dui Zhongguo gaodeng jiaoyu zhengce ji xueshu gongzuo de yingxiang" [Effect of New Public Management Concepts on Chinese Higher Education Policy and Academic Work]. *Gaodeng jiaoyu yanjiu [Journal of Higher Education Research]* 5.

Lu, N. G., and L. J. Wang. 2013. Jiaoyu gaige beijing xia de jiaoshi zhuanyexing yu jiaoshi zeren [Teacher professionalism and responsibility under education reform]. *Jiaoshi jiaoyu yanjiu [Teacher Education Research]* 1.

Ramirez, F. O. 2006. The rationalization of universities. In *Transnational governance: Institutional dynamics of regulation*, ed. M.-L. Djelic and K. Sahlin-Andersson 225–44. New York: Cambridge University Press.

Ramirez, G. B. 2013. Studying quality beyond technical rationality: Political and symbolic perspectives. *Quality in Higher Education* 19:126–41. doi:10.1080/13538322.2013.774804

Sachs, J. 1994. Strange yet compatible bedfellows: Quality assurance and quality improvement. *Australian Universities' Review* 37:1.

Salter, B., and T. Tapper 2000. The politics of governance in higher education: The case of quality assurance. *Political Studies* 48:66–87. doi:10.1007/978-1-4020-5553-9_10

Schofer, E., and J. W. Meyer. 2005. The worldwide expansion of higher education in the twentieth century. *American Sociological Review* 70:898–920. doi:10.1177/000312240507000602

Shen, W., and N. G. Lu. 2011. Wenze beijing xia de jiaoyu zhiliang: Hewei yu weihe [Education quality under accountability: What and why]. *Quanqiu jiaoyu zhanwang [Global Education]* 2.

Su, Y. J. 2013. Gaodeng jiaoyu zhiliang baozhang zhong de jiazhi chongtu yu zhenghe [Value conflict and conformity in higher education quality assurance]. *Zhongguo gaoxiao yanjiu [China Higher Education Research]* 11.

Tight, M. 2003. *Researching higher education*. Buckingham, ENgland: SRHE and Open University Press.

Trow, M. 1996. Trust, markets and accountability in higher education: A comparative perspective. *Higher Education Policy* 9:309–24. doi:10.1016/s0952-8733(96)00029-3

Trullen, J., and S. Rodriguez. 2013. Faculty perceptions of instrumental and improvement reasons behind quality assessments in higher education: The roles of participation and identification. *Studies in Higher Education* 38:678–92. doi:10.1080/03075079.2011.590587

Wang, L. J., and N. G. Lu. 2013. Jiaoyu wenze de lilun jichu yu shijian moshi: Ying, Mei, Ao san guo de kaocha [Theoretical basis and practical models for education accountability: Observations in the United Kingdom, the United States, and Australia]. *Bijiao jiaoyu yanjiu [Comparative Education Research]* 1.

Wen, J. 2012. Zhiliang wenhua diaocha: Ouzhou gaoxiao neibu zhiliang baozhang qianghua de xin lujing [Quality culture survey: A new way to strengthen internal quality assurance in European universities]. *Luoyang Shifan Daxue xuebao [Journal of Luoyang Normal University]* 6.

Xu, D. S. 2012. Pinggu yiliu de benke jiaoyu: Lujing yu jiazhi—Meiguo de jingyan ji qi yiyi [Assessing top undergraduate education: Path and values–The American experience and its significance]. *Gaodeng gongcheng jiaoyu yanjiu [Research in Higher Education of Engineering]* 3.

Yang, L. J., X. H. Yan, and Y. Q. Li. 2013. Jishu yu wenhua de ronghe: Goujian gaoxiao jiaoxue zhiliang baozhang tixi de lujing [Merging technology and culture: Building a path to a higher education teaching quality assurance system]. *Daxue (xueshu ban) [Universities (Academic Edition)]* 3.

Yorke, M. 2000. Developing a quality culture in higher education. *Tertiary Education and Management* 6:19–36. doi:10.1080/13583883.2000.9967008

Young, J. R. 2004. When good technology means bad teaching. *Chronicle of Higher Education* 12.

Zhang, M. X. 2005. Guanyu gaodeng jiaoyu renzheng jizhi de yanjiu [Research on higher education accreditation mechanisms]. *Jiaoyu yanjiu [Educational Research]* 2.

Zhang, Y. Q., and H. L. Jiang. 2013. Guanyu Zhongguo tese xiandai daxue zhidu de lilun renshi [Theoretical understanding of a modern university system with Chinese characteristics]. *Jiaoyu yanjiu [Educational Research]* 11.

Zhang, Y. X. 2012. Xin guanlizhuyi beijing xia xifang xueshu zhiye qunti de kunjing [Difficulties of western academic occupational groups under new managerialism]. *Gaodeng jiaoyu yanjiu [Journal of Higher Education Research]* 4.

Zhao, J. M. 2008. Chaoyue pinggu—Zhongguo gaodeng jiaoyu zhiliang baozhang tixi jianshe zhi shexiang [Beyond assessment–A vision for building a Chinese higher education quality assurance system]. *Gaodeng gongcheng jiaoyu yanjiu [Research in Higher Education of Engineering]* 6.

Zumeta, W. 1998. Public university accountability to the state in the late twentieth century: Time for a rethinking? *Policy Studies Review* 15:5–22. doi:10.1111/j.1541-1338.1998.tb01088.x

On the Effects, Problems, and Countermeasures of Undergraduate Teaching Evaluation in Higher Education

Liu Xianjun, Yu Yang, Zhang Junchao, Wei Shuguang, and Ding Ling

Abstract: The Undergraduate Teaching Evaluation of General Institutions of Higher Education from 2003 to 2008 was the largest-scale evaluation in Chinese higher education history. It exerted a tremendous influence as a key exploration of quality assurance with Chinese characteristics. Based on existing research, this study combines quantitative and qualitative methods to probe the evaluation's effects as well as problems and countermeasures. Major effects included establishing an undergraduate teaching baseline, fostering distinction, faculty development, teaching reform, and standardized teaching management. Problems included applying the same evaluation criteria to all institutions, unclear positioning of provincial educational authorities, weak reform efforts, inflated excellent ratings, and a timing imbalance. Suggested countermeasures include regular statutory evaluations, guidance for categorized evaluation criteria, internal quality assurance systems, teaching databases, active institutional research, and rational higher education management.

From 2003 to 2008, China's Ministry of Education organized a national undergraduate teaching evaluation of 589 institutions qualified to grant bachelor degrees prior to 2001. It was the most extensive and influential evaluation in the history of higher education in China, with the largest number of participants, nearly 10 million faculty, staff, and students. Evaluation experts including academicians from the Chinese Academies of Sciences and Engineering, university administrators, and renowned Chinese and foreign scholars made over 7,000 on-site visits to observe undergraduate teaching work. In the evaluation process, the experts made more than 50,000 classroom visits, reviewed more than 100,000 exam papers and student theses or designs, administered more than 6,000 student basic skills tests, convened 4,000 seminars and workshops, and visited more than 10,000 schools, academic departments, and functional departments within the higher education institutions. The evaluation was an important exploration of far-reaching

English translation © 2016 Taylor & Francis, Inc., from the Chinese text "Gaodeng jiaoyu benke jiaoxue pinggu de chengxiao, wenti yu gaijin duice" by Liu Xianjun, Yu Yang, Zhang Junchao, Wei Shuguang, and Ding Ling. Translated by Michelle LeSourd. Originally published in *Gaodeng gongcheng jiaoyu yanjiu* [Research in Higher Education of Engineering], 2012, no. 2.

significance to the educational philosophies and management models of institutions, and to building a quality assurance system for higher education. Nevertheless, it was subjected to more intense social debates compared to previous evaluations organized by the Ministry of Education. For such a major event in the history of higher education in China, it is significant and valuable to take a scientific approach to examine it and to reach objective and factual conclusions.

To this end, the Undergraduate Teaching Evaluation of General Institutions of Higher Education 2003–2008 Research Group carried out a study of the evaluation. Between October 2009 and February 2010, the Research Group members read more than two million Chinese characters of relevant data from the evaluation. They then traveled to 13 provinces and municipalities including Beijing, Shanghai, Liaoning, Shaanxi, and Guangdong; interviewed leaders from provincial and local education departments; made in-depth visits to nearly 50 universities to interview more than 100 administrators, 40 provosts, and 30 evaluation experts; and convened 20 forums at which more than 200 faculty members and students participated in discussions. In addition, more than 70 institutions of higher education nationwide accepted an invitation to participate in a summary and analysis of the evaluation of their schools, among which 32 institutions provided written materials to the Research Group. This study also referenced research data from the Evaluation Impact Analysis Research Group led by Professor Li Yanbao of Sun Yat-sen University (Sun Yat-sen University Group); the Evaluation Research Group led by Professor Sun Laixiang in Fudan University (Fudan University Group), and the Review and Experience Study of Chinese Higher Education Undergraduate Teaching Evaluation Group headed by Professor Liu Xianjun of Huazhong University of Science and Technology. On the basis of existing research and the principle of seeking truth from facts, this study combined quantitative and qualitative methods to conduct an in-depth analysis and summary of the background, process, effects, experiences, and problems with the evaluation, and provides references and recommendations for conducting future evaluations. The Research Group wrote a report nearly 300,000 characters in length. This article addresses the effects, problems, and countermeasures for improving upon this round of higher education evaluation.

EFFECTS OF THE TEACHING EVALUATION

The evaluation took place as China entered the massification stage of higher education, and is historically significant in terms of ensuring the quality of higher education and exploring a higher education quality assurance system with Chinese characteristics. The effects of the evaluation are described subsequently in terms of the six areas.

Transforming Institutional Ideology and Establishing the Fundamental Position of Undergraduate Education

Against the backdrop of massification, internationalization, and an increasing use of information technology in China's higher education system, new situations and problems have arisen in education and teaching management that destabilize the fundamental position of undergraduate teaching in institutions of higher education. The evaluation was aimed at transforming the

21

educational philosophy, increasing funding for education, encouraging faculty to value under-graduate teaching, and creating a good atmosphere in which everyone focuses on teaching and on students. It was meant to encourage institutions to transform their guiding institutional ideology and reinforce the fundamental position of undergraduate education.

Transforming the Educational Philosophy

The institutions participating in the evaluation engaged in extensive discussions of their educational philosophies based on the Evaluation Program's provisions on "Transforming educational philosophy and establishing the central position of teaching." Through such discussions, the institutions deepened their understanding of the importance of training high-quality talent and of the central position of teaching. When the Fudan University Group surveyed administrators, school and department heads, evaluation experts, and renowned professors in Shanghai, Wuhan, and Dalian, 58.71% of respondents believed that the evaluation played a significant role in enhancing the fundamental position of undergraduate teaching. Institutions of higher education generally made undergraduate teaching their "number one" project, which was personally responsible by the school's Party secretary and president. The institutions used a series of measures, including teaching meetings, administrators participating on the front lines of teaching and spearheading teaching research, and research-based teaching practices to enhance the fundamental position of undergraduate teaching.

Increasing Education Funding

The evaluation spurred governments and institutions to focus on education funding, with parti-cular emphasis on tilting the internal allocation of funds within institutions toward teaching. Governments at all levels were encouraged to gradually increase education funding each year. During the early stage of massification, state education funding as a proportion of the total budgets of general higher education institutions dropped year by year, from 58.16% in 2000 to 42.86% in 2006. Although the level of government investment in higher education funding remains unsatisfactory, the growth rate improved a great deal as the evaluation progressed. For example, in 2008 the national expenditure on education was 1.450074 trillion yuan, an increase of 19.37% over 2007s 1.214807 trillion yuan. Within that amount, the state education budget was 1.044963 trillion yuan, an increase of 26.20% over 828.021 billion yuan in 2007. Education spending in the higher education institutions' per-student budgets in 2008 grew an average of 15.76% over 2007. There was a large increase in the number of students during the evaluation period but, beginning in 2006, as the number of students continued to grow, average funding per student increased annually, reaching 7,577.71 yuan in 2008.

Meanwhile, under the impetus of the evaluation, higher education institutions did everything possible to cut costs and raise funds. For example, they accessed special state funding and raised operating funds by engaging in school-run industries and logistical and social services, and solicited donations from businesses and alumni. In response to the Evaluation Program's requirements for the "four expenses" (the operating expenses, education travel, physical education support, and teaching equipment maintenance of undergraduate and polytechnic institutions) as a proportion of tuition income, participating institutions optimized their outlay structures, controlled administrative expenditures, prioritized teaching expenditures, and

TABLE 1

Percentage of Total Investment in the "Four Expenses" as Proportion of Annual Tuition Income (Selected Institutions)

Institution	2004	2005	2006
Peking University	32.50	35.50	41.20
Tsinghua University	41.13	42.57	45.64
Fudan University	40.53	46.32	52.07
University of Science and Technology Beijing	28.80	31.60	32.30
Beijing Institute of Technology	27.35	31.94	34.89
Shanghai University of Finance and Economics	26.83	32.25	35.48
Beijing University of Chinese Medicine	25.83	27.09	30.34
Ocean University of China	32.67	35.12	38.33
Beijing Sport University	34.27	38.37	45.24
South China University of Technology	26.47	29.03	31.77
China University of Political Science and Law	28.85	31.19	32.01
Qinghai University	25.88	26.84	29.47
Ningxia University	25.19	30.61	37.65
Central Academy of Fine Arts	28.55	33.18	37.35
Central Academy of Drama	30.56	32.15	40.77
Hebei University	30.10	30.46	31.22
Yan'an University	28.20	30.11	33.06
Shandong University of Technology	27.43	30.16	31.62
Huaihai Institute of Technology	25.81	28.44	33.37
Kashgar Teachers College	15.02	18.38	23.49
Xinjiang University of Finance and Economics	20.25	25.10	30.33

Source: Data consolidated from the 2007 self-assessment reports of selected participating institutions.

increased the funding for teaching. During the evaluation, the ratio of the "four expenses" to tuition income increased year by year (see Table 1), which basically ensured demand for teaching expenditures.

Encouraging Faculty to Value Undergraduate Teaching

To improve the quality of undergraduate teaching and ensure its central position, the Evaluation Program was used to guide and encourage faculty to value undergraduate teaching. First, the proportion of professors and associate professors teaching undergraduates gradually increased. This was accomplished by standardizing a system for professors and associate professors to teach undergraduates, while also creating conditions facilitating their entrance into the undergraduate classroom. As a result, the proportion of professors and associate professors teaching undergraduates increased each year (see Table 2). Second, a tutoring system was implemented for undergraduates. To strengthen the guidance of undergraduates in their thinking, learning, and life, some institutions systematically required full-time instructors to be responsible for advising a certain predetermined number of undergraduate students. Third, scientific research was used to promote teaching. Many institutions promoted teaching by bringing research into the classroom, promoting growth through the practice of research, using research funding to aid teaching, and engaging in collaborative research to build bridges.

TABLE 2
Proportion (%) of Professors & Associate Professors Teaching Undergraduates (Selected Institutions)

Institution	Academic year 2004–2005	Academic year 2005–2006	Academic year 2006–2007
Zhejiang University	75.48	81.99	85.90
Xi'an Jiaotong University	85.11	85.49	86.05
Shanghai University of Finance and Economics	96.80	97.30	98.00
China University of Political Science and Law	92.37	93.58	96.69
Ningxia University	95.00	95.50	99.09
Qinghai University	82.10	86.30	95.10
Tibet University	85.60	94.40	100.00
Hebei University	96.20	96.10	99.60
Shenzhen University	95.32	95.83	100.00
China Pharmaceutical University	95.45	96.24	98.16
Beijing Film Academy	95.00	99.00	100.00
Central Academy of Fine Arts	97.41	97.78	98.53
Jiangxi University of Finance and Economics	97.70	98.10	98.80
Jilin Agricultural University	97.05	99.32	100.00
Yangtze University	96.70	98.62	99.09
Henan University	94.15	95.02	95.01
Guangdong University of Business Studies*	96.94	97.18	97.23
Guangdong Ocean University	97.00	95.60	97.80
Guangdong University of Technology	92.80	96.30	98.40
Hebei University of Science and Technology	96.46	97.78	100.00
Hainan Normal University	95.30	97.30	100.00

Source: Data consolidated from the 2007 self-assessment reports of selected participating institutions.
Translator's note: It was renamed Guangdong University of Finance and Economics in 2013.

Reviewing the Past, Planning for the Future, and Fostering Unique Characteristics

The evaluation spurred participating institutions to review the past and plan for the future. It was the first such comprehensive round of review and planning among Chinese universities in a century of history, and was widely acknowledged by both faculty and students. During the survey, a university president said with deep feeling: "The evaluation has prompted us to conscientiously review our own educational history and do something great for the future development of our institution, which we always wanted to do but had not done."

Clarifying the Institutions' Educational Philosophies

Reviewing an institution's educational history and streamlining its thinking is actually a process of testing and refining its educational philosophy. It is a gradual process of unifying thinking and understanding, thereby building up an educational philosophy. The survey results from the Sun Yat-sen University Group indicate that 69% of respondents believed that the evaluation process had a significant impact on the institution reviewing its history, streamlining its thinking, and refining its characteristics. Based on its own unique circumstances, each institution engaged in study and discussions, and achieved significant results. High-level universities clarified their guiding institutional ideologies and objectives; institutions with solid foundations and long histories clarified their educational philosophies; newly established and merged institutions further unified their educational philosophies and streamlined their thinking.

Assisting the Institutions to Position Themselves Appropriately

An appropriate position is the premise and basis for the good management of a college or university. Especially in a highly competitive society, only when such an institution finds its own place in society can it remain immune to competition. During the evaluation process, each participating institution engaged in a series of Party, faculty, and staff assembly meetings, teaching conferences, and discipline development conferences to benefit from collective brain-storming. Based on the requirements of the evaluation indicators, each gradually developed its position based on the features of the times and its own unique characteristics, thereby driving forward the institution's self-development. An analysis of interviews at 50 colleges and universities reveals that the evaluation encouraged key national universities in China's 985 and 211 programs to clarify their own social responsibilities and enhance their sense of historical mission, providing guidance for comprehensive institutional development. For local institutions, it enhanced their close links with regional economic development and improved their overall strength and reputation. During discussions to establish the position of each institution, a number of innovations also emerged, such as the teaching intensive and service-oriented university. They explored the connotation and institutions for such institutional positioning from numerous angles.

Reviewing and Developing the Institution's Unique Characteristics

The Evaluation Program addressed "characteristics projects," and made clear that institutions deemed excellent in the evaluation must have "distinctive characteristics," while those deemed good institutions must have a "characteristics project." This requirement prompted each participating school to recognize and summarize their own characteristics, and enhanced their awareness of such characteristics. This was very valuable work with far-reaching significance for the reform and development of higher education in China. In a nationwide survey of 102 outstanding faculty, 78 believed that the evaluation greatly contributed to participating schools refining their own unique characteristics. The conclusion based on the interviews also reveals that the evaluation encouraged administrators and faculty to think more deeply about their institution's features and school traditions, and to tap into its individual characteristics. Specifically, institutions with longer histories used that foundation to innovative new ideas and summarize and refine their characteristics projects; some newer undergraduate colleges and universities were able to use a brainstorming process to clarify a direction for developing their own characteristics and establishing characteristics projects.

Improving Infrastructure and Conditions to Provide a Good Educational Environment

After the expansion of student enrollment at China's colleges and universities, their basic teaching conditions and resources were unable to keep up with the pace of the expanding enrollments or to meet teaching requirements, seriously constraining and affecting teaching quality. Each requirement put forward by the Evaluation Program prompted participating institutions to do everything possible to enhance their development. As a result, teaching conditions improved significantly.

Marked Improvements to Basic Teaching Facilities and Environment

The evaluation played a major role in promoting the development of teaching conditions that essentially met the needs of institutions after the expansion of enrollment in 1999 (Shi and Yuan 2008). The improvements to school buildings, laboratories, and practicum and internship facilities were the most notable, providing a solid material foundation and good educational environment to ensure and improve teaching quality. Specifically, in 2003, after the evaluation has been launched and as the number of students increased each year, the per-student size of classrooms, dormitories, and physical education facilities increased to some degree and basic teaching infrastructure improved markedly. By 2007, the overall floor area of higher education institutions nationwide had increased by 312.8601 million square meters over 2002, a 100% increase. Classroom floor area in 2007 increased 62.4328 million square meters over 2002, or 0.52 square meters per student. Dormitory floor area grew by 96.1684 million square meters in 2007, 1.29 square meters per student more than in 2002. The floor area of physical education facilities in 2007 increased by 9.5876 million square meters over 2002, or 0.21 square meters per student.

Substantial Achievements in Developing Teaching Resources

Developing teaching resources is an important condition for ensuring high-quality teaching. Institutions focused on building up teaching and research equipment by increasing investment, integrating resources, improving equipment utilization, and other measures, and achieved fruitful results. For example, between 2003 and 2006, the per-student area of teaching and administrative buildings, dormitories, and physical education facilities among the 133 colleges and universities participating in the evaluation in 2006 all grew by more than 20%. The value of per-student funding in the "four expenses," the number of computer stations per 100 students, and teaching and research equipment per student in these institutions all increased by more than 30%. The growth in the number of multimedia classroom and language laboratory seats per 100 students and annual book acquisitions per student all exceeded 60%. Among the 198 institutions participating in the evaluation in 2007, between 2004 and 2007, per-student investment in the "four expenses" increased by more than 27%, and the per-student value of teaching equipment grew by more than 33%. The value of teaching and research equipment assets at general institutions of higher education in 2007 increased by 98.1899199 billion yuan over 2002; there were 2.8096 million units of computers in 2007 compared to 2002; language laboratory seats in 2007 increased by 75.16 million over 2002 while multimedia classroom seats increased by 9.9333 million; and in 2007, paper books increased by 759.0333 million and e-books by 556.9322 million over 2002 (Ministry of Education 2002–2007).

Major Improvements in Laboratory Conditions

Participating institutions invested heavily in the construction of lab facilities, and laboratory conditions were greatly improved. When undertaking the evaluation, to improve the quality

TABLE 3
Teaching Laboratories at General Institutions of Higher Education, 2002–2007

Year	Labs/practice sites			Teaching & research equipment assets		
	Size (1,000 m²)	Per student (m²)	Growth over prior year (%)	Value (million yuan RMB)	Per student (RMB)	Growth over prior year (%)
2002	40,836.7	4.52	–	62,547.5862	6,923.58	—
2003	57,009.0	5.14	39.60	81,129.1624	7,318.16	29.71
2004	64,194.2	4.81	12.60	101,793.7262	7,633.59	25.47
2005	75,835.5	4.86	18.13	121,683.5906	7,791.36	19.54
2006	87,468.8	5.03	15.34	142,407.5755	8,189.78	17.03
2007	96,439.6	5.12	10.26	160,737.5061	8,527.66	12.87
Avg growth rate	–	4.91	19.19	–	7,730.69	20.92

Sources for data in **Tables 3–5**: Ministry of Education (2002–2007).

of undergraduate teaching, institutions focused on building advanced electrical engineering, chemical engineering, mechanics, computer science, physics, and other teaching laboratory centers. They also prioritized building basic experimental teaching centers in the arts and humanities. Such centers at some schools covered all common and basic courses, specialty foundation courses, and specialty courses throughout the institution in the sciences, engineering, arts and humanities, law, economics, management, and other domains. This created a fully equipped experimental education system and institutional management mechanism with a reasonable level of teaching resources. Building such laboratories improved experimental teaching conditions and met the fundamental needs of students for lab teaching. It is evident from the table of teaching laboratory conditions at general institutions of higher education (see Table 3) that laboratory and internship space increased by 55.6029 million square meters between 2002 and 2007, with an average annual growth of 19.19%. The value of teaching and research equipment assets increased by 9,818.9999 million yuan during the same time period, an average annual growth rate of 20.92%. Institutions also worked to build more internship sites to meet teaching practice needs. To ensure a steady improvement in the teaching quality of practicum activities, they focused on building laboratories and teaching centers inside the school, but also maximized the integration of external resources and establishing practice bases outside the school to enrich the institution's teaching resources.

Intensified Development of Information Technology and Creation of Digital Campuses

Participating institutions made efforts to build excellent campus websites and develop digital campuses. The numbers of computer stations, language laboratory seats, and multimedia classroom seats per student, as well as the number of online courses, increased significantly over 2002. In that year, general institutions of higher education offered an average of only 12 online courses; after the implementation of the evaluation, the number continually increased until 2007, when the average number reached 34, three times that of 2002 (Ministry of Education 2002–2007). Meanwhile, the evaluation encouraged institutions to establish modern academic management systems, implement information-based management, and use their campus websites to provide comprehensive services to undergraduate teaching.

Enhancing Faculty Development to Ensure Teaching Quality at the Source

As enrollment in Chinese colleges and universities continued to expand, they were unable to meet basic requirements for faculty quantity and quality. At the same time, as vast numbers of students poured into the institutions, the number of younger faculty grew rapidly, which exacerbated the issue of the academic and campus atmosphere. Faced with these problems, participating schools worked to safeguard the quality of teaching at the source by increasing the number of faculty, improving faculty structure and quality, and strengthening professional ethics.

Increasing the Number of Faculty

The student-to-teacher ratio is the primary means of determining whether the number of faculty is sufficient. In 1998, the student-to-teacher ratio at China's undergraduate education institutions was 11.63 to 1. After the country entered the massification stage of higher education, the ratio reached 20.66 to 1 in 2002 and 21.07 to 1 in 2003. At certain schools, the ratio went as high as 83 to 1. In view of this situation, the Evaluation Program provided clear requirements for the student-to-teacher ratio in undergraduate teaching. To reduce the ratio, participating schools adopted various recruiting measures to reach a significant increase in the number of faculty. In 2002, the total number of faculty at general institutions of higher education nationwide was 618,400, which nearly doubled to 1.1683 million in 2007, an increase of 549,900 (see Table 4).

Improving Faculty Composition

Faculty composition directly affects the teaching quality. The Evaluation Program therefore contained specific requirements for faculty composition. The composition of full-time faculties at general institutions of higher education, in terms of their educational qualifications, was thereby greatly improved. In 2002, there were 43,400 faculty members with doctoral degrees, accounting for 7% of all faculty. Those holding postgraduate degrees totaled 192,800, or 31% of the total. In 2007, there were 132,300 faculty holding doctorates, or 11.32%, while those with postgraduate degrees numbered 507,300, 43.4% of the total. By 2007 the proportion of faculty with postgraduate degrees increased by 11.4% over 2002 (see Table 5). At the same time, faculty composition in terms of academic origin[1] and job titles also improved to some extent.

TABLE 4
Full-Time Faculty by Rank in General Institutions of Higher Education, 2002–2007 (1,000 Persons)

Year	All full-time faculty	Professors	Associate professors	Lecturers
2002	618.4	60.2	186.3	211.0
2003	725.0	70.1	216.2	240.6
2004	858.0	83.2	250.3	280.9
2005	966.0	96.6	278.2	312.0
2006	1,076.0	108.9	304.8	1,352.2
2007	1,168.3	119.7	326.3	394.4

28

TABLE 5

Full-Time Faculty by Degree at General Institutions of Higher Education, 2002–2007 (1,000 Persons)

Year	Total full-time faculty	PhD		Master		Baccalaureate	
		n	%	n	%	n	%
2002	618.4	43.4	7.02	149.4	24.16	397.3	64.25
2003	725.0	53.6	7.39	182.5	25.17	458.5	63.24
2004	858.0	70.5	8.22	223.9	26.10	532.7	62.09
2005	966.0	88.5	9.16	269.0	27.85	578.4	59.88
2006	1,076.0	108.6	10.09	317.8	29.54	620.2	57.64
2007	1,168.3	132.3	11.32	375.0	32.10	725.5	62.10

Improving Overall Faculty Proficiency and Quality

Institutions participating in the evaluation generally viewed faculty quality as the most important aspect of their institution development, and undertook various measures to guide faculty to improve their academic standards and teaching proficiency. During interviews, administrators and faculty both affirmed from different angles the role of the evaluation in improving the overall proficiency and quality of faculty. Many schools used the policies of "active recruiting, large-scale training, optimizing the composition, and enhancing proficiency" to take every possible measure to improve overall faculty quality and proficiency. For example, they assisted faculty in laying out their own growth and development plans through practice; used mentoring by older faculty, teaching seminars, teaching supervision, observation of lectures, and short-term training to improve the teaching proficiency and quality of younger faculty; recruited and cultivated high-level academic leaders; and implemented study abroad programs.

Significantly Improving Professional Ethics, Teaching Style, and Academic Atmosphere

The evaluation played an important role in promoting the formation of excellent academic atmospheres, teaching styles, and campus atmospheres. A university president said during an interviews that "building a first-class university involves many factors, but the chief among them is the culture of the university, developing its unique style, temperament, and traditions by gradually summarizing and refining its own history; it is the social character of the school. The evaluation had an important role in spurring institutions to refine themselves further to develop their own styles and create good campus atmospheres, academic atmospheres, and teaching styles." The engagement and dedication of faculty was significantly enhanced as the evaluation was used to drive institution development. During numerous student discussion forums convened by the Research Group, participating students indicated that, motivated by the evaluation, faculty invested more effort in teaching, which significantly enhanced their teaching effectiveness. At the same time, institutions seized the opportunity of the evaluation to use their past experience and fine school traditions as a foundation for taking effective measures, using constraints or incentives and other means to improve the academic atmosphere and have it permeate the school's education and teaching activities.

Engaging in Teaching Reform and Improving the Quality of Talent Development

Teaching reform is a long, complex process that requires the unremitting efforts of several generations. Although this round of evaluation did not achieve a breakthrough in teaching reform, it laid a good foundation for future, deeper reform by actively exploring curriculum system reform, building a quality curriculum, and practice teaching.

Strengthening the Development of Specialties

Specialties (majors) are the vehicles for talent development. The schools placed particular emphasis on adjusting their specialty structure based on societal requirements, relied on the development of disciplines to enhance their specialty level, and placed great importance on starting new specialties. First, they adjusted their specialty structures according to the needs of society. During the evaluation process, institutions of higher education organized personnel to visit companies, businesses, schools, and governments to research and understand society's demands for talent, and then made timely adjustments to optimize their specialty structures. Second, they turned their discipline advantages into specialty advantages. Disciplines are the foundations for specialties, and specialties represent the application of academic disciplines. Disciplines and specialties both have a talent development function, both are associated with certain knowledge, and both rely upon a certain organizational structure. Some universities with good discipline foundations began to explore integrating the development of specialties and disciplines, turning their discipline advantage into specialty advantage, and worked to develop unique specialty characteristics and train high-quality talent. Third, they intensified their efforts to develop new specialties. In recent years, due to social development requirements, colleges and universities have generally added a large number of new specialties. The presence of such new specialties have had a direct impact on the quality of talent development. The Evaluation Program put forth explicit requirements regarding newly established specialties, weighting the issue to spur institutions to place a high degree of concern and emphasis on new specialties.

Exploring Talent Development Models

The presence of a single, outdated talent development model is a major problem constraining the development of human resources in China. Many colleges and universities have recognized the seriousness of this problem. The evaluation prompted institutions to strive for the "top-down design" of talent development and continually improve their talent development programs. In addition, they actively explored new talent development models and worked to design and test innovative, entrepreneurial models consistent with the laws of scientific and technological development and the laws of talent growth.

Initiating Curriculum System and Content Reform

The structure and quality of the curriculum determines the quality of specialty development as well as student training. With regard to curriculum, the Evaluation Program put forward specific requirements in terms of teaching content and curriculum system reform, developing and selecting teaching materials, teaching method and strategy reform, and bilingual education. The Sun

Yat-sen University Group's survey results indicate that more than 90% of respondents believed that the evaluation played a significant role in promoting the reform of curriculum systems, teaching content, and teaching methods. The evaluation spurred institutions to undertake curriculum system reform, develop quality curricula, and strongly emphasize practice teaching.

Strengthening Institutional Development and Standardizing Teaching Management That is Suited to the Institution

During discussions of the evaluation and its impact on their institutions, many administrators, school and department heads, and faculty invariably used the word "standardization" in their responses. In the Sun Yat-sen University Group survey, when asked about the greatest area of the evaluation's impact, 90.53% of respondents chose the "standardization of teaching management," which demonstrates that the evaluation was extremely important in propelling schools to strengthen their institutional development and standardize their management practices.

Developing Teaching Systems

The renowned educator John Amos Comenius pointed out that systems are the "soul" of a school's work: "Where the system is stable, everything is stable; where the system is shaky, everything is shaky; where the system is undisciplined, everything is undisciplined and chaotic" (Comenius 1990). Strengthening teaching and improving the quality of education must also rely on systems. China's colleges and universities, however, have long been weak on documentation, systems, and standardization. Existing systems are outdated, incomplete, and not well adapted to the new era of higher education; in addition, systems are lacking—appropriate systems have not been established for the many new things in educational reform and development; and finally, systems are not implemented and exist in name only. Participating institutions undertook great efforts and achieved relatively good results in changing this situation. During interviews, schools of all types generally stated that their development of systems was strengthened through the evaluation. Institutions in the 985 program indicated that the evaluation motivated them to further refine and standardize the teaching management of schools and departments. Institutions in the 211 program stated that their teaching management standards were improved by means of the evaluation. They built stronger teaching management teams, and understanding and communication between faculty and administrators became smoother. Local and newer undergraduate institutions generally believed that the evaluation provided specific guidance for building new undergraduate programs and establishing teaching management standards. Administrative department heads believed that the evaluation spurred their institutions to establish and strengthen teaching management systems, along with quality assurance monitoring mechanisms.

Establishing Internal Quality Assurance Systems

There are internal and external higher education quality assurance systems. External quality assurance uses laws, regulations, national standards, and external evaluations to realize government macromonitoring and assurance of higher education. Internal quality assurance is an institution's own mechanism to guarantee the quality of education and establish internal quality control and improvement. The institutions of higher education themselves are the primary quality assurance entities; the purpose of an external evaluation is to promote the development of an institution's internal quality assurance system. Each institution must actively develop an internal system to promote the creation of long-term internal quality assurance mechanisms based on its own actual conditions as well as national standards. The evaluation effectively prompted institutions of higher education to establish internal quality assurance systems.

Strengthening Teaching Management Teams

Attaining a high level of teaching management requires a high-quality teaching management team. The evaluation prompted institutions to concentrate their efforts on teaching management team-building and establish combined full- and part-time teaching management teams with rational staffing structures, personnel stability, high quality, and a strong sense of service. First, they created a more rational structure for the institution's teaching management team. Next, they enhanced the professional quality and service awareness of teaching management personnel. Nearly 90% of faculty and students expressed a positive attitude toward these points during their interviews. Finally, institutions established more advanced teaching management methods and improved efficiency.

The evaluation not only achieved significant results, but also accumulated certain experiences, as described subsequently. Conducting regular evaluations according to law and using teaching evaluation as a starting point is an effective way to impact teaching quality in higher education during the massification stage. It is necessary to adhere to the guidance of the *Twenty-Word Guidelines*[2] and the *Three Correspondences*[3] to promote scientific development and foster distinction among institutions of higher education. Persisting in the rational development of evaluation programs and using a combination of quantitative and qualitative assessment methods are important ways to improve the objectivity and efficacy of evaluations. Important safeguards of evaluation success include sticking to the core work of improving teaching quality, focusing on benefiting students, and using research alongside practice. These experiences provide a valuable resource from which we can draw lessons for future evaluation work and building a higher education quality assurance system with Chinese characteristics.

PROBLEMS WITH THE TEACHING EVALUATION

The undergraduate teaching evaluation achieved significant results, essentially reached its goals, and accumulated important experiences, but a number of problems persist that we must continue to improve and perfect in future evaluations.

Using the Same Evaluation Criteria for All Participating Institutions and Insufficient Guidance for Categorized Evaluations

With regard to problems in the evaluation, survey results from the research groups around the country indicate that about 90% of respondents believed the greatest problem was the evaluation's use of the same criteria for all participating colleges and universities. There was no guidance for categorization based on the different levels and types of institutions. The community also generally agreed that using the same evaluation criteria for different levels and types of institutions, and with different discipline structures, easily led to inappropriate competition among these institutions and caused the evaluation process and conclusions to deviate from the original intent and objectives.

At the same time, we must take note of the significant regional differences between higher education institutions in China. Government investment in higher education differs between regions because of gaps between their economic development levels. For example, there is a large gap between the education conditions and faculty resources of colleges and universities in western and eastern China, due to the constraints of long-term geographic factors and local economic development. There is a similarly large gap between local colleges and universities and institutions directly funded by the central government, but within the same region, in terms of resources and education conditions. Local colleges and universities tend to have innately weak foundations; they are bound to expend more energy and funds to achieve the same conditions as higher-status institutions. The design of future evaluations should use criteria adjusted based on regional economic differences to reduce the pressures on institutions themselves and on local governments.

Unclear Position of Provincial Education Departments; Insufficient Community Participation

The evaluation was primarily organized, promoted, and implemented by the Ministry of Education. As is typical for a government evaluation of colleges and universities, it was quite authoritative. During the evaluation process, however, the position of the provincial education authorities was not defined, which led directly to blind competition between provincial education departments, and in turn to competition between provinces to obtain excellent evaluation ratings. At the same time, the evaluation did not fully mobilize the enthusiasm and role of the provincial education authorities, and their involvement was insufficient. Their role was limited to cooperating with the Ministry of Education's Higher Education Evaluation Center and the teams of experts visiting the campuses. This is incompatible with establishing a system of higher education "managed by the central and provincial People's Governments, primarily planned and managed at the provincial level." Provincial education departments are actually most familiar with the higher education situation in their provinces. Appropriately sparking their enthusiasm for the work will greatly enhance the effectiveness of higher education evaluations.

Although experts, members of the community, employers, faculty, and students participated in the evaluation to a certain extent, in general it was strongly dominated by the administrative viewpoint, and there was not enough participation from the various sectors of the community. An evaluation is both a value judgment and a collective building of values. The government, society, and students are qualified to be involved in evaluations, both in making value judgments and in building values. Creating a mechanism for community participation in evaluations is an inevitable historical trend and an inevitable choice. From an international point of view, comprehensive theories have already been developed regarding the evaluation of higher education, and it has its own special methods. It will be possible, when conditions are ripe, to move toward professionalized evaluation, so that higher education evaluation in China truly becomes a normalized, professional, authoritative accrediation for higher education quality. We can also gradually develop a higher education quality assurance system with Chinese characteristics.

Weakness in the Reform Phase; Lack of Effective Mechanism for Reform Supervision and Follow-Up

During the evaluation process, many colleges and universities were fully aware of the importance of reform work to consolidate the results of the evaluation, and of building long-term mechanisms to ensure teaching quality. They also undertook effective measures to ensure that their reform work would achieve tangible results. Nevertheless, some institutions were relatively weak in terms of the reform portion compared with their self-evaluation and the external evaluation by an expert group. First, they failed to fully recognize the importance of reform work. They believed that, when the expert group completed their on-site observation, it meant the end of the evaluation, and they did not broaden their thinking to include reform. They did not consider the significance of reform work in terms of their institution's long-term development or that of higher education as a whole. Second, they lacked mechanisms for reform supervision and follow-up. At the conclusion of the expert group's on-site observation, the Ministry of Education required participating institutions to submit reform proposals as soon as possible to its Higher Education Evaluation Center and the Department of Higher Education. After one year of reform, they were to submit a report on their progress to the Department of Higher Education. Due to a lack of follow-up, and of supervision and restraint mechanisms, the reform work at some colleges and universities was a mere formality, which impacted the effectiveness of the evaluation at those institutions.

Inadequate Organization and Management, Inflated Excellent Ratings, and Imbalance in Timing

There were two main problems with the organization and management of the evaluation: inflated excellent ratings, and an imbalance in the timing of the evaluation. These two issues directly affected the credibility of the evaluation's conclusions, which become a focus of public attention.

Various segments of the community generally believed that the over-use of excellent ratings was one of the problems with the evaluation. In 2003, 46.7% of participating institutions received a rating of excellent; in 2004 the proportion was 55.6%; in 2005 it was 57.3%; in 2006 it was 75.2%; in 2007 it was 80.8%; and in 2008 the proportion was 81.6%. The inflated excellent ratings led the community to question the reliability of the evaluation findings, and they were also inconsistent with actual developments in Chinese higher education.

Rating the participating institutions as excellent, good, qualified, or unqualified did not serve the purpose of the evaluation, nor did it conform to the actual conditions at colleges and universities. Compounded by the inflation of excellent ratings, this resulted in serious consequences. A strong desire to excel led some institutions to engage in fraudulent behavior, which corrupted their campus and academic atmospheres. A "campaign-style" approach was developed, bent on achieving quick success; after the evaluation, some institutions then relaxed their efforts. There was a tendency toward a gradually increasing formalism, which consumed a great deal of human and material resources. An accurate understanding and in-depth analysis of the inflated excellent ratings will provide a valuable reference and inspiration for future evaluations of undergraduate education institutions.

The evaluation also lacked rational timing. It was loose at the beginning and tight at the end, and advanced too quickly during the latter portion in particular. There were 589 colleges and universities that actually participated in the evaluation, which meant, based on the five-year evaluation period, that an average of 118 institutions were evaluated each year. The scale of the evaluation was immense. Moreover, the evaluation proceeded at imbalanced speeds. In 2003, 42 institutions were evaluated; in 2004, the number was 54; in 2005, it was 75; 133 institutions were evaluated in 2006, 198 in 2007, and 87 institutions were evaluated between January and July of 2008. During the first two years of the evaluation, fewer than 100 institutions were evaluated, but in 2007 alone the number was nearly 200. Such an intensive and fast-paced evaluation is bound to result in simplified and hasty organization and management, and omissions and confusion in certain areas, thereby affecting the scientific nature and rigorousness of the conclusions.

COUNTERMEASURES SUGGESTED FOR FUTURE EVALUATIONS

The undergraduate teaching evaluation took place during the initial massification stage of higher education in China. It was a significant initiative taken to address a decline in the quality of higher education. The evaluation was a useful exploration of developing a higher education quality assurance system with Chinese characteristics. A comprehensive summation of lessons learned from this round of evaluation, and an in-depth analysis of the problems that arose, are important prerequisites for persisting and continuing to improve China's evaluation system.

Persist in Regular Statutory Evaluations, Continue to Center on Teaching Evaluation, and Gradually Improve the Evaluation System

For future evaluations, we must draw from the experience of this evaluation round and obtain a profound understanding of its problems, in order to continue to conduct evaluations according to law and to perfect our evaluation methods, criteria, and mechanisms. While the government organizes and manages the evaluations according to the law, we must also actively create the conditions to foster the development of a variety of evaluation entities and gradually establish a mechanism for the participation of multiple subjects in the evaluation, thereby creating a good atmosphere for all of society to focus on and ensure the quality of higher education. In macro terms it means, in the greater context of developing higher education, establishing external teaching evaluation mechanisms, internal institutional teaching quality assurance systems, and effective societal monitoring mechanisms. In micro terms, it requires the participation of personnel from different areas of the community in the expert groups to allow them to understand the institutions and to increase the transparency of higher education, thereby achieving positive interactions between the schools and society.

Future evaluations should continue to revolve around evaluating teaching. The evaluation achieved notable results, and played an important role in teaching quality assurance during the initial massification stage of higher education. Nevertheless, the problems of inadequate investment in higher education and the inability of teaching quality to meet the needs of social development have not yet been fundamentally resolved. To ensure the basic work of teaching quality assurance in higher education, teaching must remain the focus of the work of colleges and universities; it continues to be the most basic element at this stage of quality assurance.

Appropriately Position and Increase the Participation of Provincial Education Departments, Offer Guidance for Categorized Evaluation Criteria, and Make Evaluation More Relevant and Rational

Evaluation is an effective way for education authorities at all levels to actively adapt to changes in the external governance structure, respect and expand the autonomy of higher education institutions, and move from a focus on "process management" toward "management by objectives" to achieve macrolevel control. Future evaluations should be planned and coordinated by the Ministry of Education, but the provincial education departments must play a much greater role. The future evaluation trend in China should be that the management functions of state education authorities over higher education institutions are gradually transformed from administrative management to macromanagement through legislation, funding, and other methods as necessary. Through the development of regulations on higher education evaluation policy, the government can establish quality standards and make its primary task the macromanagement, coordination, and supervision of the evaluation work. Meanwhile, with the advent of intermediary evaluation entities, the government can fully play its role and take its rightful place in the macromanagement and supervision of such intermediaries.

The standards for future evaluations should include guidance for categorized evaluations to continuously improve the focus and rationality of evaluations. The scale of talent development at different levels and types of institutions is not the same, and society has different demands for human resources. Therefore, while adhering to the same evaluation program, there must also be guidance on how to categorize the evaluations. Only in this way can we encourage institutions to enhance their quality and foster distinction to meet the diverse requirements of society. At the same time, we can try using an audit-style model to evaluate the institutions participating in the last round of evaluation. The evaluation cycle could be extended as appropriate. For newer colleges and universities, we can try out an accreditation-style model that primarily observes basic school conditions, administrative standards, and teaching management. The evaluation cycle could be shortened as appropriate. In addition to institutional evaluations, we should also make better use of specialty (major) evaluations and thematic evaluations. Meanwhile, to address the different development levels of institutions in different regions of China, we can try using the same expert group to observe colleges and universities in the same region. This will aid in achieving more scientific and objective conclusions.

Prioritize Internal Quality Assurance Systems and Long-Term Mechanisms for Teaching Quality Assurance

Evaluation is an effective means of promoting the development of teaching conditions, the reform of education and teaching, and the improvement of quality talent development at institutions of higher education. While external evaluation is a driving force, institutions must create their own self-development and self-restraint mechanisms in order for teaching evaluation to become conscious behavior, which will better promote the sustainable development of the institution. External quality assurance pushes institutions to build internal, long-term mechanisms for undergraduate teaching quality. Evaluations of undergraduate teaching are used to establish internal self-monitoring and assurance mechanisms to improve teaching quality, as well as adaptive mechanisms ready to accept external inspection and evaluation at any time, so that undergraduate teaching evaluation gradually becomes a natural part of the school's teaching work.

Build Basic Teaching Databases and Encourage Broad Community Participation in Evaluations, Actively Undertake Institutional Research, and Promote Rational Management

Society is becoming increasingly concerned with the quality of higher education and teaching, and institutions are creating and improving databases on the basic state of their teaching. These developments will effectively aid in providing a format for evaluations, while also offering the most direct route to broad societal participation in the evaluation process. We must therefore continue to build and improve basic teaching databases and to publicize the relevant data, allowing the community to know more about institutional operations and achieving better social monitoring. At the same time, the use of such databases will usher in a new stage of institutional research promoting scientific management, and will provide decision support for such management. In future evaluations, we must vigorously promote institutional research to drive progress in the scientific management of colleges and universities.

NOTES

1. Translator's note: Academic origin refers to the proportion of faculty who obtained the same or similar degrees from different schools or research institutions. It addresses a common phenomenon at Chinese academic institutions in which students do their undergraduate through doctoral work at the same institution, often studying while teaching part-time, and then remain at that institution as faculty members. The phenomenon has been blamed for insularity and lack of innovation.
2. Translator's note: The guidelines specify using the evaluation for development, reform, innovation, and standardized management; combining the evaluation with teaching reform and long-term development; and staying focused on institution-building.

3. Translator's note: The degree to which an institution's goals correspond to actual social requirements and conditions at the school, to which the actual work of the institution corresponds to its goals, and to which the quality of its talent development corresponds to its goals.

REFERENCES

Comenius, J. A. 1990. *Kuameiniusi jiaoyulun zhuxuan* [Selected works of Comenius on education] (B. X. Ren, trans.), 242. Beijing: People's Education Press.

Ministry of Education. Zhongguo jiaoyu tongji nianjian [China Education Statistical Yearbook]. 2002–2007. Beijing: People's Education Press.

Shi, C., and J. T. Yuan. 2008. Zhongguo gaoxiao benlun jiaoxue pinggu de yiyi yu pingjia [Assessment and significance of the current teaching evaluation of Chinese colleges and universities]. *Jiaoyu yu zhiye* [Education & Vocation], 12, 31–33.

The Effectiveness of the Higher Education Quality Assessment System: Problems and Countermeasures in China

Zhou Guangli

Abstract: The effectiveness of the higher education quality assessment system is essentially a matter of policy evaluation. On the macro level, such a system refers to external quality assessment, which includes government evaluation, quality certification, and university rankings. Depending on the degree of government intervention, the external quality assurance system can take the form of either accreditation or certification. China's first undergraduate teaching evaluation was essentially a government-led accountability system for higher education institutions, known as administrative accountability. The first round of evaluation was basically recognized and considered moderately effective, but left great room for improvement. To improve the quality assessment system for higher education in China, a social accountability system must be established.

As higher education has developed worldwide since the 1950s and 1960s, it has been transformed from elite higher education to mass higher education. The massification of higher education has brought increased attention to the issues of higher education quality and standards. The Declaration of the World Conference on Higher Education clearly stated, "In the 21st century, there will be more emphasis on quality and a transition from quantity to quality, signaling the end of one era and the beginning of another. Focusing on quality is the proposition of the era. Those who neglect quality will pay a heavy price." As the new century began, higher education in China also entered a rapid massification stage. With the massification, internationalization, diversification, and individualization of higher education, building a higher education quality assessment system has increasingly become a focus of public attention.

English translation © 2016 Taylor & Francis, Inc., from the Chinese text "Gaodeng jiaoyu zhiliang pinggu tixi de youxiaoxing: Zhongguo de wenti yu duice" by Zhou Guangli. Translated by Michelle LeSourd. Originally published in *Fudan jiaoyu luntan* [Fudan Education Forum], 2012, vol. 10, no. 2, and funded by the National Social Science Foundation 11th Five-Year Plan 2008 Education General Topic "Effectiveness of China's Higher Education Quality Assessment System in Light of Social Accountability" (BIA20080027).

OVERVIEW

In developed Western countries, research on the effectiveness of higher education quality assessment systems began in the 1980s and 1990s. In the West, quality assessment systems have become a stable and recognized part of the higher education system, and related practical and theoretical research is on the rise. Current research in the West focuses mainly on the following questions. (1) How do we evaluate the work of scholars operating in the "quality industry"? (2) What form of quality assurance system is best for higher education? (3) Are the degree standards in specific higher education systems all the same? Do they always remain the same? (4) What is the role of performance-based funding systems? (5) How can the results of quality assurance practices most effectively be conveyed to users of higher education? (6) What is the relationship between evaluation, criteria, and quality? (Tight 2003). These questions actually all point to the question of the effectiveness of the higher education quality assessment system. Since Western scholars have not formed a universally applicable view of higher education quality, research on the effectiveness of quality assessment systems in higher education is still in its infancy. As Malcolm Tight, Donald Houston, and other scholars have pointed out, "Understanding the quality of higher education is bound to affect the means of assuring quality and the methods for assessing quality. While most attention, as we have seen, has been given to the quality assurance systems in actually in use—often transferred, with relatively little thought, from manufacturing and service industries—some academics have argued for the introduction of particular systems for the higher education quality assurance" (Tight 2003).

China's focus on quality assessment system's effectiveness originated from its expansion of higher education enrollment and launch of a comprehensive undergraduate teaching level evaluation. At the turn of the new century, China's massive enrollment expansion sparked concerns about a decline in higher education quality. To ensure and improve the quality of higher education, the Chinese government launched a five-year round of undergraduate teaching level evaluation. At present, research in China on quality assessment system effectiveness revolves around examining this undergraduate teaching evaluation at colleges and universities. For the most part, people make subjective judgments about the effectiveness of the undergraduate teaching evaluation from the perspective of personal experience. There are two main viewpoints. Government officials and evaluation experts adopt a positive attitude in confirming the outstanding achievements of the undergraduate teaching evaluation and its positive impact on institutions. They believe that the existing assessment system is effective on the whole, and therefore advocate continuing with the present system while improving and enhancing it.

In contrast, some scholars, teachers, students, media workers, and others in the community take a negative stance in criticizing and reflecting upon the undergraduate teaching level evaluation. They believe that the existing system needs to be made more effective. Although some of them have advocated the extreme position that the evaluation should be canceled, most people still believe that, to improve the effectiveness of future assessments, intermediary education agencies should implement such assessments, with the addition of multi-party participation. Exactly what are the characteristics of China's higher education quality assessment system? Is it actually effective? How can we improve it? This article is a re-examination of these questions from the perspective of social accountability.

THEORETICAL FRAMEWORK

The effectiveness of an assessment refers to the degree to which the intended purposes of the assessment are realized after its implementation. Scholars have different interpretations of this concept. One view is that the effectiveness of an assessment is equivalent to the validity of that assessment, or to what extent the assessment measured what it intended to measure, reflecting the degree of its authenticity and accuracy. The effectiveness of an assessment is closely related to its objectives; the results of an evaluation survey must be consistent with its objectives to be effective. Based on this viewpoint, Deng Guosheng and Xiao Mingzhao propose a theoretical framework in which people assess the effectiveness of the government. This analytical framework includes four phases and five factors. The first is the data gathering and assessment phase. The key factors impacting effectiveness in this phase are the objectivity and fairness of the assessment's findings. Findings feedback is the second phase. The key factor in this phase is the usefulness and operability of the assessment's findings. The third is the findings utilization phase. The key factor for effectiveness here is the government's use of moderate pressure at the time that the assessment's findings are applied. Response to the findings is the fourth and last phase. The key factor in this phase is whether the evaluated institutions can improve the timeliness and effectiveness of their response to the findings, and whether all stakeholder groups can truly benefit from the assessment process (Deng and Xiao 2006).

Another view is that effectiveness refers to the capacity of the assessment system to produce results, and to whether the objectives are realized. This viewpoint stresses that the goal of the assessment is not only to measure quality; more importantly, it is to improve and enhance quality. The key to an effective assessment is to create a plan of action to which most stakeholders can agree. Accomplishing this involves continuous consultations and negotiations, on the basis of respect for a variety of values, so that stakeholders can find reasons to support the program and actively seek to implement it.

Trudy W. Banta developed a number of characteristics of effective assessment based on the phases of planning, implementation, and improving and sustaining. First, in the planning phase, an effective assessment enables stakeholder participation to reflect their interests and needs and obtain their support; is used as a tool for improvement and does not terminate when the assessment activities end; and has clear objectives that relate to people's values. Second, during the implementation phase, an effective assessment uses knowledgeable and effective leadership; recognizes that the assessment promotes learning and makes it everyone's responsibility; develops a sense of responsibility for the assessment at each unit level; focuses on both the findings and the process of the assessment; and conducts the assessment in a receptive, supportive environment. Third, in the improving and sustaining phase, an effective assessment produces valid evidence of learning and of organizational effectiveness; ensures continual use of the assessment data to improve services and specialties; provides evidence to demonstrate to those inside and outside the organization; creates expectations that performance assessment will be ongoing; and integrates continual assessment with improving the assessment itself (Zhao 2009). The core concept of such an effective assessment is to promote comprehensive and active participation, which requires stakeholders and other related persons to be on an equal footing in the assessment. Politically, they must be treated as full equals throughout the assessment program's design, implementation, interpretation, and ultimate findings phases.

In terms of philosophy, the first view treats assessment as a purely scientific process, which is supported by a positivist paradigm. Under this paradigm, there are certain objective realities in the quality issue. When knowing an object, the knower must maintain an objective distance, eliminate subjectivity, and ultimately obtain scientific data. This paradigm ignores the issues of social, political, and value orientation in conducting assessments.

The second view treats an assessment as a process of social construction, which is supported by an interpretivist paradigm. Under this paradigm, what we know as reality is essentially composed of a series of mental constructions. A quality survey cannot ignore the subject's values, and must recognize the influence of those values on the survey. The positivist paradigm gives priority to those who commission the survey, because they can give or deprive stakeholders of certain rights by selectively releasing the assessment findings. "If information is power, then information withheld is power reduced. If clients have the final word on what information will be released, to whom, when, and by what means, the process is clearly tilted toward the maintenance and even enhancement of power for those who already possess it, while depriving the relatively powerless of even that little that they have" (Guba and Lincoln 1989).

The interpretivist paradigm advocates equality for the assessment stakeholders, which requires full consideration of different values and giving the stakeholders capacity and power. An assessment following the positivist paradigm adheres to the logic of managerialism, and its corresponding policy framework is an administrative accountability system. In such a system, assessment follows the traditional paradigm of "those responsible respond." The manager is the accountable entity, and the managed are the recipients of the accountability; the two are separated. Managers often refuse to self-reflect and do not accept criticism. Those managed often fall into "accountability phobia" as agents of the manager. On-site evaluators, under the pressures of this environment, often collude with managers, unable to hold their own in the role of evaluator. There are two main disadvantages to such an accountability system. First, it often leads to unfavorable comparisons and unhealthy competition. The accountability object tends to focus on the outcome indicators, and may even engage in opportunistic behavior to achieve a "good" evaluation. Second, the system ignores the views, concerns, and arguments of stakeholders.

The interpretivist paradigm adheres to the logic of public governance, and its corresponding policy framework is a social accountability system. Under such a system, the assessment emphasizes the initiative of the accountability object, which consciously assumes responsibility. The evaluators and the evaluated interact during the accountability process, identifying their problems and concerns; stakeholders are periodically provided with relevant, timely, and effective information; and a communication platform is established to allow stakeholders frequent opportunities to express their views and participate in the accountability process and outcomes. The most important purpose of accountability under this system is not proof, but improvement, to help institutions to make decisions that meet the needs of stakeholders while providing performance accountability information.

Assessment is essentially a process with social and political overtones. We should view society, culture, and politics as the most fundamental characteristics of the human environment and integrate them into the assessment process. Assessment is a process of cooperation among stakeholders. During an assessment, all constructs, viewpoints, concerns, and arguments should be equally laid out, understood, and criticized, so that consensus can be achieved on at least the areas of agreement, to form a common construct. Assessment is also a teaching and learning process; the evaluation process promotes learning on the part of both the evaluating entity and the stakeholders. The evaluating entity helps each stakeholder to clarify their own construct while they also learn about various different viewpoints. As the survey proceeds, they continue to introduce new constructs and allow stakeholders to communicate about them, so that each person's construct is rebuilt. The effectiveness of an assessment is realized not only in the promotion of quality improvement; more importantly, it gives rise to conceptual changes. From a social accountability point of view, an effective assessment uses negotiation to allow stakeholders to achieve a more informed and complex construct than ever before. To improve its effectiveness, China's higher education quality assessment system must therefore make strategic adjustments to move from the positivist paradigm to the interpretivist paradigm—from administrative accountability to social accountability.

DESCRIPTION

Higher education quality assessment refers to judging the quality of the educational activities of higher education institutions. When such an institution is the object, an assessment coming from outside the institution is an external evaluation, while an assessment coming from the institution inside is an internal evaluation. Generally, it is difficult for an internal evaluation to have a positive effect without external pressure. External evaluation is therefore a core component of a quality assessment system. The higher education quality assessment system that we examine here refers to systematic, normalized, and institutionalized external quality assessment. The external quality assessment system in China consists of three main components: accreditation, certification, and social assessment. Accreditation is an administrative assessment led by the government, mainly at the time the college or university is established. The government develops specific and relatively stringent standards for the establishment of higher education institutions, and individuals or organizations planning to establish such institutions submit applications to the government. The government puts the applications through various forms of close scrutiny, and ultimately approves the establishment of the institutions (Xu 2007). This type of assessment is characterized by a relatively stringent review on the establishment of an institution, but relatively relaxed administrative supervision afterward.

Certification is an assessment by an intermediary organization. It uses higher education establishment and access standards developed by community groups, and only colleges and universities that comply with such standards are determined to be qualified. Under this form of assessment, the certification for establishing an institution is not very strict, but it must be re-certified on a regular basis (every five years). There are two types of certification. One is implemented by nongovernmental organizations (the American style), and the other is implemented by a quasigovernmental agency (the British style).

Social assessment, also known as diversified market assessment, is represented primarily by college and university rankings. This type of assessment is designed to adapt to the diverse needs of diverse subjects in the higher education market. It uses language that the public understands to identify core elements of higher education quality. Social assessment focuses on examining the school's reputation, and is not regarded as the most effective quality assurance method. Accreditation and certification are the two fundamental assessment systems for modern higher education.

Quality Accreditation System of China's Higher Education

In 1986, the State Education Commission issued the *Interim Regulations on Establishing General Higher Education Institutions*, which signaled the establishment of China's higher education accreditation system. These regulations set standards for management personnel, faculty, school conditions, library resources, school funding, and other aspects of higher education, and stipulated the processes for approval and acceptance. This type of assessment system originated in the ancient education licensing system, which originated during the Middle Ages in Europe. Institutions were issued licenses by the pope or a secular king to acknowledge the school's qualifications. This was the earliest meaning of "accreditation." After the establishment of a university, the king or pope regularly or occasionally went to the school to make an inspection, and sometimes bestowed a financial gift; this was the usual oversight and supervision (Xu 2007). In 1991, the State Education Commission promulgated the *Interim Provisions on Educational Supervision*, which provided for systematic, routine government inspections of higher education institutions. Under China's higher education accreditation system, a relatively stringent review takes place when an institution is established but, once established, the administrative supervision is relatively relaxed. In recent years, with the massification of Chinese higher education, routine supervision under the accreditation system has become increasingly strict. The accreditation bodies, once government agencies, have become quasigovernmental entities. Their assessment findings have received more and more attention. China's higher education system is gradually moving into an era of assessment.

In fact, the Decision of the Central Committee of the Communist Party of China on the Reform of the Education System proposed the idea of education assessment in 1985. In 1990, the State Education Commission issued the Interim Provisions on Education Assessment of General Higher Education Institutions, which for the first time provided for the quality assessment of general (nonvocational) institutions of higher education. The regulations made specific provisions regarding the nature, purpose, mission, guiding ideology, and basic format of assessments. These were the first series of important regulations in China on higher education quality assessment and assurance. In 1998, the Higher Education Law was promulgated, marking the first legislation of higher education assessment in China. Article 44 of the law provides that "higher education institutions should accept supervision and evaluations of their school management and education quality organized by the education administrative departments." In the 2003 Action Plan for Rejuvenating Education 2003–2007, the Ministry of Education (MOE) specified the implementation of a teaching level evaluation system for general institutions of higher education "every five years." In addition to implementing a comprehensive assessment of colleges and universities, the Chinese government launched a series of specialized assessments, including the National Evaluation of Graduate Schools at General Higher Education Institutions, the Evaluation of Doctoral and Master Degree Granting Institutions, the Selective Evaluation of Level I Disciplines, the Basic Qualifications Evaluation of Doctoral and Master Degree Granting Institutions, and the National Outstanding Doctoral Dissertation Awards.

Quality Certification System of China's Higher Education

Assessment and certification by intermediary organizations were first developed in the United States. In an accreditation system, colleges and universities need not worry about securing resources and quality assurance, because they are guaranteed by the credibility of the government. In a certification system, the government is not responsible for the quality assurance of institutions. Higher education institutions must therefore create certification organizations themselves to demonstrate the quality and level of their education and research to society (Xu 2007).

In China, the conditions are not yet ripe for nongovernmental organizations to establish education certification bodies. The most likely future certification entities will be quasigovernmental agencies. The 2003 *Action Plan* formally proposed implementing a teaching level evaluation system for institutions of higher education every five years. The plan included standardizing and improving teaching quality evaluations of disciplines and specialties, and gradually establishing a specialty evaluation system linked to the personnel credential certification and vocational access systems. It was actually a signal that China would establish a specialized certification system. Specialized certification is targeted at specialty education programs and designed to determine whether such programs meet minimum educational standards. A certification system that observes and examines a school's overall situation, to determine whether it meets minimum education standards, has not yet put on the agenda in China. In recent years, Chinese institutions have been keen to establish various higher education alliances, including the C9 League, the Shanghai Southwest Area University Consortium, the Cooperation Consortium of Universities in Wuhan, and the Northern League (*Beiyue*) and China League (*Huayue*) autonomous enrollment consortia, to name a few. Because they are constrained by narrow utilitarian considerations, it is difficult for such consortia to survive over the long term. Establishing an education quality certification consortium may perhaps be a new way to begin developing higher education alliances in China.

Social Assessment System of China's Higher Education Quality

University rankings are a concentrated expression of the social assessment system for higher education in China. The 1985 *Decision of the Central Committee* provided an institutional space for the ranking of colleges and universities in China. Higher education ranking then really took off after the establishment of the socialist market economic system. In 1992, the State Council approved the *State Education Commission Opinion on Accelerating Reform and Actively Developing Higher Education*, which required that "society must actively support and directly participate in assessments of the establishment, talent development, management, and educational quality of higher education institutions." In 2002, the MOE and the Ministry of Science and Technology (MOST) emphasized in the *Opinions on Fully Developing the Role of Higher Education Institutions in Scientific and Technological Innovation* that colleges and universities should make full use of their technological and talent advantages to establish and foster independent, community-based, intermediary scientific assessment bodies to conduct science evaluations. In May 2003, the MOST, the MOE, the Chinese Academy of Sciences, the Chinese Academy of Engineering, and the National Natural Science Foundation jointly issued the *Decision on Improving Science and Technology Evaluation*. In September of that year, the MOST formulated and promulgated the *Measures for the Evaluation of Science and Technology (Trial Implementation)*. This series of policy documents essentially became the policy basis for college and university ranking assessments by both the government and nongovernmental entities. In September 1987, the Scientific Research Institute of the China Academy of Management released the first university rankings in China. According to incomplete statistics, from that time to the present nearly 20 entities in China have publicized more than 30 rankings of different types and levels of colleges and universities.

It should be noted here that the appearance of higher education rankings broke the previous government monopoly on higher education assessment; it was beneficial to establishing a market-oriented higher education assessment system and spurred institutions to become more market-oriented. The greatest advantage of college and university rankings is that they use language the general public understands to assess the quality of higher education, and have achieved a high degree of social acceptance. Nevertheless, such rankings have also led to numerous controversies and doubts, and they face the challenge of a credibility crisis. The challenge is that the ranking entities lack authoritativeness and credibility; the ranking indicator system is not entirely scientific or rational; and the data sources are not very reliable and lack the support of a public, systematized database.

ANALYSIS AND DISCUSSION

Our empirical survey of the effectiveness of China's first undergraduate teaching evaluation showed the following results: 40% of those surveyed believed the level of effectiveness was "fair," while only a combined 24% gave "good" and "very good" ratings. The "poor" effectiveness rating comprised 24%, and the proportion giving a "very poor" rating was higher at 36%. A total of 76% rated the effectiveness fair or below, which points to a lack of optimism about the effectiveness of China's accreditation-style assessment system (Zhou and Zhou 2012).

In this regard, scholars have put forward two basic paths to reform. One is to retain the status quo and continue with government-organized assessments; the other is to turn the assessments over to society. Because the two paths address the issue in terms of a single subject, however, they both face the possibility of "assessment failure." Although the public recognizes government-based assessment to a certain degree, it has also been criticized. At the same time, while public calls for nongovernmental assessment have gradually grown louder, there remain doubts about that path. The government is a single evaluation subject; it does not allow for the participation of various sectors of society, and thus fails to meet the diverse needs of the public. The community has therefore called for intermediary agencies to implement such assessments, with the joint participation of multiple stakeholders. Because Chinese civil society is not well developed and lacks a public higher education data system, it is difficult for the public to obtain accurate and complete information from colleges and universities. Meanwhile, the government is likely to use executive power to obtain such data. Moreover, a reverence for the position of officials is deeply entrenched in Chinese culture, and the public therefore has more faith in the government than in civil society. In view of such conditions in China, it is undesirable to use any form of single-subject assessment to build an effective higher education quality assessment system. The only rational choice is to integrate several assessment subjects in a diversified, comprehensive assessment system that is government-led, but allows for public and community participation. This has been the successful experience of some developed countries in building a higher education quality assessment system.

From the perspective of accountability, the Chinese undergraduate teaching evaluation was typical of administrative accountability: it was vertical and top-down, and the grassroots level of society did not participate. They are absent in advance of or during the assessment process, and only get involved into the stage of after evaluation. In this stage, the assessment findings are made public and accept social supervision. Nevertheless, this is only symbolic social participation. Since there is no way for the public to participate, such assessments cannot substantially constrain or influence institutions of higher education. The public must be allowed to truly become involved with, produce a substantial impact on, and function to prod colleges and universities; social accountability will then become an ideal path to reform. As a World Bank expert group said, "Social accountability relies upon citizen participation to strengthen administrative accountability; it directly or indirectly promotes administrative accountability through ordinary citizens or civil society organizations." We can see that social accountability is a form of cooperation between government and society regarding higher education accountability. It is not a unilateral action by either the government or society.

The core of a social accountability system is an accountability body composed of both internal and external stakeholders of higher education institutions. It operates under government guidance, coordination, and certification, and is organized by the government and other social assessment entities together. Higher education stakeholders effectively participate throughout the process, resulting in an integrated accountability arrangement. The factors involved in higher education social accountability include the accountability subject, object, content, methods, and procedures. The accountability subject refers to the entity that, during the accountability process, raises some kind of challenge or interest demand to institutions of higher education, and to which the institutions must respond. A diverse group of higher education accountability subjects should be established, such as People's Congresses, governments, government agents or entities, funding organizations, intermediary organizations, student-related organizations, donors, alumni, parents, employer-related organizations, sponsoring entities, professional organizations, teacher-related organizations, and business and industry.

Defining the accountability object addresses the question of "who is accountable." For social accountability in higher education, those accountable are primarily the colleges and universities themselves. Accountability content, also known as the scope or matter of accountability, addresses the question of "for what are they accountable." This includes education, management, teaching, research, faculty, students, and many other details. It can be reflected specifically in student characteristics, costs and financial assistance, the number of new student and transfer applications, the number admitted and enrolled, the numbers of degrees and research fields, institutional characteristics, and the results of student experience surveys and student learning assessments. Accountability procedures actually refer to "how to pursue accountability," and usually include launching the accountability activities, organizing and presenting information, participation and feedback, processing the findings, making remedies and improvements, and supervising implementation. The various reports, surveys, rankings, budgeting, funding, evaluation, and publicizing information online are specific accountability methods of operation.

Another important issue is what kind of role the public plays in a social accountability format involving public participation in higher education quality assessment. At present, at least three roles are equally important. The first is stakeholders commenting as survey respondents, including student experience surveys and surveys of graduates. The second is public participation on teams of experts to directly evaluate colleges and universities. The third is members of the public participating as supervisors in all phases of the assessment, which increases the integrity of behavior on the part of both institutions and evaluation teams. Of course, the timely release of assessment findings to the public is a minimum requirement and also very important.

CONCLUSION

China's current system of higher education quality assessment consists of government-led accountability of higher education institutions; this form of accountability is not highly effective. Nevertheless, assessments purely organized by civil society are not realistic, either. Only by moving toward a broader and more inclusive higher education social accountability system, and establishing a system in line with China's national conditions, will it be possible to fully mobilize the enthusiasm and initiative of higher education stakeholders to participate in the management and supervision of colleges and universities. This is the only way to improve the credibility of quality assessment, which will ultimately enhance the effectiveness of China's higher education quality assessment system.

REFERENCES

Deng, G. S., and M. Z. Xiao. 2006. *Qunzhong pingyi zhengfu: Lilun, fangfa yu shijian [The masses appraise government: Theory, methods, and practice]*, 31. Beijing: Peking University Press.

Guba, E. G., and Y. S. Lincoln. 1989. *Fourth generation evaluation*, 9–10. Newbury Park, CA: Sage Publications, Inc.

Tight, M. 2003. *Researching higher education*, vol. 111, 127. Berkshire: Open University Press.

Xu, G. X. 2007. *Riben gaodeng jiaoyu pingjia zhidu [Study of the Japanese higher education assessment system]*, vol. 8, 10. Hefei: Anhui Education Press.

Zhao, L. Y. 2009. Meiguo boshisheng peiyang zhiliang pinggu youxiaoxing yanjiu [Study of the effectiveness of American doctoral education quality assessment]. Diss., Huazhong University of Science and Technology, 73–74.

Zhou, G. L., and X. L. Zhou. 2012. *Zhongguo gaodeng jiaoyu zhiliang pinggu tixi youxiaoxing yanjiu—jiyu shehui wenze de shijiao [Effectiveness of China's higher education quality assessment system: From the social accountability perspective]*, 127. Changsha: Hunan People's Publishing House.

Newly Built Undergraduate Schools Should Place Great Emphasis on Connotation Construction and Quality Promotion: An Analysis Based on the Qualification Evaluation Results for 41 Undergraduate Schools

Zhong Binglin

Abstract: The article presents a quantitative analysis of the evaluation results for 41 newly built undergraduate schools that submitted to the qualification evaluation of undergraduate work by Ministry of Education in 2013. It shows that newly built undergraduate schools should place great emphasis on connotation construction and quality promotion and on updating their concepts of education and exploring multiple talent cultivation models. They should improve their human resource and material resource building, explore innovation of internal systems and mechanisms, create a good campus culture and educational atmosphere, and continually improve their level of teaching and quality of talent cultivation.

In January, 2015, the Undergraduate Education Evaluation Expert Committee of Ministry of Education held a work meeting and deliberated the qualification evaluation reports on 41 newly built undergraduate schools that submitted to the qualification evaluation of undergraduate education work in 2013, (Zhong 2012a) and formed evaluation conclusions through anonymous voting. These results elicited a large response in the world of higher education. The author has conducted a quantitative analysis of the on-campus inspection evaluation results of the Qualification Evaluation Expert Groups of Ministry of Education,[1] and on this basis I offer policy recommendations for the reform and development of newly built undergraduate schools in the hopes of benefiting the connotation construction of newly built undergraduate schools.

STRUCTURAL ANALYSIS OF THE EVALUATED SCHOOLS

In 2013, 41 newly built undergraduate schools submitted to on-campus inspection by the Ministry of Education Qualification Evaluation Expert Groups. The regional distribution of

English translation © 2016 Taylor & Francis, Inc., from the Chinese text "Xinjian benke yuanxiao yao gaodu zhongshi neihan fazhan he zhiliang jianshe—jiyu 41 suo benke yuanxiao hege pinggu jieguo de fenxi" by Zhong Binglin. Translated by Jeff Keller. Originally published in *Zhongguo gaojiao yanjiu* [China Higher Education Research], 2015, no. 06.

TABLE 1
Regional Structure Analysis for Evaluated Schools

	Eastern region	Central region	Western region	Subtotal
Number of schools	13	17	11	41
Proportion	31.7%	41.5%	26.8%	100.0%

TABLE 2
Nature Structure Analysis for Evaluated Schools

	Public schools	Private schools	Subtotal
Number of schools	30	11	41
Proportion	73.2%	26.8%	100.0%

TABLE 3
Category Structure Analysis for Evaluated Schools

	Comprehensive	Science and engineering	Finance and economics	Politics and law	Language	Education	Medicine	Subtotal
Number of schools	21	5	5	3	1	4	2	41
Proportion	51.2%	12.2%	12.2%	7.3%	2.4%	9.8%	4.9%	100%

the schools was 13 in the eastern region, 17 in the central region, and 11 in the western region (see Table 1). The nature of the schools was 30 public schools and 11 private schools (see Table 2). The school categories were 21 comprehensive schools, five science and engineering schools, five finance and economics schools, three politics and law schools, one language school, four education schools, and two medical schools (see Table 3). On the whole, a full range of school categories participated in the evaluation and the coverage was broad, so to a certain extent analyzing the evaluation results of these 41 schools is representative.

ANALYSIS OF THE WORK VOLUME OF THE EXPERT ON-CAMPUS INSPECTIONS

In 2013, the Ministry of Education organized 41 Qualification Evaluation Expert Groups of undergraduate education work to inspect campuses. According to the student size and subject structure of the evaluated schools, each expert group consisted of seven to nine people, and a total of 346 expert visits were made. Before the experts visited the campuses, they reviewed the school self-evaluation reports and basic education status data analysis reports and formulated campus evaluation plans. On the campuses they used methods such as file reviews, classroom observations, brief visits, in-depth interviews, and communication evaluations to perform comprehensive, detailed inspections of school education work and give opinions and feedback. After leaving the schools the experts made evaluation reports individually and as a group. At the 41 schools the experts listened to a total of 1,209 classes, reviewed 51,689 tests, reviewed 31,034 graduate theses (design projects), visited 1,710 school administration departments and education units, inspected 168 off-campus internship bases and employment units, and conducted 4,444 in-depth interviews (see Table 4).

TABLE 4
Expert On-Campus Inspection Work Volume Analysis

Inspection Content	Work volume	Per-school work volume
Class observation (classes)	1,209	30
Test review (test)	51,689	1261
Graduate thesis (design project) review (theses)	31,034	757
Visiting school administrative departments and education units (units)	1,710	42
Visiting off-campus internship bases and employment units (units)	168	4
In-depth interviews (person-times)	4,444	108

On the whole, the expert group on-campus inspections had full content, multiple methods, broad coverage, and high work volume. During their on-campus inspections the experts focused their efforts, worked diligently, grasped a large volume of first-hand information, understood the current state of education work at the school, experienced the schools' campus, learning, and cultural atmospheres, and laid a solid foundation for objectively evaluating and correctly diagnosing education work at these newly built undergraduate schools.

ANALYSIS OF MAIN OBSERVATION POINT EVALUATION RESULTS

The undergraduate education work qualification evaluation indicator system covers the entire process of and all main segments of the talent cultivation of undergraduate students. It is the basis for schools facilitating construction through evaluations and expert groups conducting on-campus inspections and also a comprehensive review and inspection of education work at newly built undergraduate schools. The indicator system includes seven level-one indicators, 20 level-two indicators, and 39 main observation points (40 observation points for private schools), as shown in Table 5.

The data analysis results show: among the 39 main observation points (40 for private schools), all the evaluated schools were fully qualified in 17 points, and about two thirds of these main observation points centered on the two level-one indicators "construction of learning atmosphere and student guidance" and "teaching quality." Of the remaining 22 (23 for private schools) observation points, 10 observation points (11 for private schools) had three schools that were not qualified, which was less than 8% of the evaluated schools. There were four schools not qualified for 12 observation points, which exceeded 10% of the evaluated schools. Of these, there were 11 schools that were not qualified for five observation points, which exceeded one quarter of the evaluated schools. Table 6 lists the analysis results for the 12 main observation points that occurred more frequently among the unqualified evaluated schools.

Analyzing Table 6 tells us the following:

1. More than four fifths of the evaluated schools were not qualified for the observation point "faculty team structure," with a failure rate of 80.5%. Of these, only 2 of the evaluated private schools passed, and the failure rate was 81.8%. The failure rate for public schools was 80.0%, which was not significantly different than that for private schools. The data analysis results show: the problem of faculty team construction for newly built undergraduate schools has already become a "bottleneck"

TABLE 5
Qualification Evaluation Indicator System of Undergraduate Education Work in General Higher Education
Institutions

Level-one indicators	Level-two indicators	Main observation points (each)
1. Guiding institutional ideology and leadership role	1.1 School orientation	1
	1.2 Leadership role	2*
	1.3 Talent cultivation model	2
2. Faculty	2.1 Quality and structure	2
	2.2 Education and teaching level	2
	2.3 Cultivation and training	1
3. Teaching conditions and utilization	3.1 Basic teaching facilities	3
	3.2 Expense investment	1
4. Specialties and curriculum	4.1 Specialty construction	2
	4.2 Curriculum and teaching	2
	4.2 Practical teaching	4
5. Quality management	5.1 Teaching management team	1
	5.2 Quality monitoring	2
6. Construction of learning atmosphere and student guidance	6.1 Construction of learning atmosphere	3
	6.2 Guidance and service	2
7. Teaching quality	7.1 Moral education	2
	7.2 Professional knowledge and ability	2
	7.3 Physical and aesthetic education	1
	7.4 On- and off-campus evaluation	2
	7.5 Employment	2

*There are 40 qualification evaluation indicator system observation points for private undergraduate schools, and the additional observation point is leadership role.

restricting connotation construction and sustainable development for schools, and in particular faculty team structure urgently needs optimization.

2. More than two fifths of the evaluated schools failed in the observation point "production-study-research cooperation education," with a failure rate of 43.9%. There was not a great difference between public and private schools, as the failure rates were 43.3% and 45.5%, respectively. The data analysis results show: newly built undergraduate schools need to further clarify their guiding institutional ideology, continually deepen reforms of talent cultivation models, actively explore new models of school-business cooperation and production-study integrated learning, and continually improve the cultivation quality of applied and technical talents.

3. More than two fifths of the evaluated schools failed in the observation point "specialty setup and structure adjustment," with a failure rate of 41.5%. Public schools had a failure rate of 41.5%, which was greater than the private school rate of 36.4%, and the difference was rather significant. The data analysis results show: newly built undergraduate schools should meet the needs of economical and social development and truly improve specialty construction work. In particular, public schools need to further change their conceptions, improve their specialty setup, adjust their specialty structures, and build platforms for improving the talent cultivation quality.

TABLE 6
Ranking of Nonqualified Observation Points of the Evaluated Schools (First 12)

No.	Main observation points	Level-two indicator affiliated	Number of nonqualified schools	Ratio of evaluated schools	Number of public schools	Ratio of public schools	Number of private schools	Ratio of private schools
1	Faculty team structure	2.1	33	80.5%	24	80.0%	9	81.8%
2	Production-study-research cooperation education	1.3	18	43.9%	13	43.3%	5	45.5%
3	Specialty setup and structure adjustment	4.1	17	41.5%	13	43.3%	4	36.4%
4	Quality control	5.2	15	36.6%	11	36.7%	4	36.4%
5	Cultivation and training of teachers	2.3	11	26.8%	5	16.7%	6	54.5%
6	Construction and use of lab practice site	3.1	7	17.1%	4	13.3%	3	27.3%
7	Graduate thesis (design project) and comprehensive training	4.3	6	14.6%	4	13.3%	2	18.2%
8	Structure and quality of teaching management team	5.1	6	14.6%	4	13.3%	2	18.2%
9	Student-teacher ratio	2.1	5	12.2%	4	13.3%	1	9.1%
10	Experimental education	4.3	5	12.2%	3	10.0%	2	18.2%
11	Construction and use of library, materials and campus network	3.1	4	9.8%	4	13.3%	0	0
12	Teaching expense investment	3.2	4	9.8%	3	10.0%	1	9.1%

4. More than one third of the evaluated schools failed in the observation point "quality control," with a failure rate of 36.6%. The difference between public and private schools was not significant, as the failure rates were 36.6% and 36.4%, respectively. The data analysis results show: newly built undergraduate schools need more scientific and standardized teaching management, the building of internal education quality monitoring and assurance systems has already become a weak procedure in school education and talent cultivation work, and in particular, quality assurance systems urgently need to be more effective.

5. More than one quarter of the evaluated schools failed in the observation point "cultivation and training of teachers," with a failure rate of 26.8%. Of these, more than half of private schools failed, as their failure rate was 54.6%, and it was only 16.7% for public schools, so the difference was extremely significant. The data analysis results show: newly built undergraduate schools, in particular newly built private undergraduate schools, must place great emphasis on the cultivation and training of faculty, improve faculty cultivation and training planning, adopt truly feasible measures, and improve the overall quality of their faculty teams.

6. The failure rates of the evaluated schools for "construction and use of lab practice site"; "graduate thesis (design project) and comprehensive training"; "structure and quality of teaching management team"; "student-teacher ratio"; "experimental

education"; "construction and use of library, materials and campus network"; and "teaching expense investment" were all above or around 10%. This should strongly attract the attention of university and local education administration authorities. They should use targeted improving measures for the sake of realizing overall improvement results.

7. There were one to three evaluated schools that respectively failed in the 11 observation points "ideology of talent cultivation"; "practical training"; "employment quality"; "dorm, athletic venue, activity site, and construction and use of facilities"; "cultivation plan"; "teaching content and curriculum resource construction"; "school orientation and planning"; "education level"; "professional theory and techniques"; "employment rate"; and " leadership system of private universities," with a failure rate less than 8% (not included in the table). Relevant universities should pay close attention to this and adopt corresponding measures for improvement.

TRULY GET A GRASP OF EDUCATION WORK OF NEWLY BUILT UNDERGRADUATE SCHOOLS

Performing a quantitative analysis on the evaluation results of the 41 newly built undergraduate schools that submitted to qualification evaluations of undergraduate education can provide important enlightenment and lessons for developing newly built undergraduate schools. I believe that both schools that passed qualification evaluation and those that have not yet passed, both schools that already underwent qualification evaluation and those that are preparing to undergo it, and both public and private schools must further increase their sense of urgency and responsibility, focus their efforts on talent cultivation and education work, and truly grasp connotation development and quality promotion for their schools. I therefore propose the following countermeasure recommendations:

Update Education Concepts

First, newly built undergraduate schools must establish student-based education values for facilitating comprehensive student development, follow the rules of education and talent growth, focus on character-building education work and all other work, and form a campus culture that values talent cultivation and education work. Second, they must re-establish views of talent that are suitable to the present age, rebuild diverse quality views that follow the development rules in the stage of mass higher education and the demands for economic and social development, break through the confines of the traditional cultivation model of "a thousand schools that all look the same" and "ten thousand people who all look the same," respect students' right to choose, encourage students to follow their interests and strong points, and explore cultivating student diversity and individuality. Third, they must uphold a student-centered learning view in their education activities, do away with old education views centered on teachers, textbooks, and classrooms, change the roles of teachers, build student-teacher learning communities, explore advanced teaching and study methods, improve student-teacher interaction and student cooperation, encourage students to independently and cooperatively study, and continually improve student learning results. Fourth, they must establish a scientific development view, persist in development that coordinates size, structure, quality, effectiveness, and speed (pace), adjust and optimize structure, improve quality effectiveness, and grasp development pace all while appropriately expanding size, and promote the healthy, sustainable development of schools.

Explore Diverse Talent Cultivation Models

First, define talent cultivation objectives and specifications. Newly built undergraduate schools should earnestly study the new challenges to talent cultivation brought by economic, social, scientific, and technical development (Zhong 2013). They should incorporate the positioning of school development objectives and outstanding education features and define the school's talent cultivation objectives for all specialties based on the diverse demands of national and local economic and social development for different types and levels of advanced professional talents. They should study student knowledge, ability, and quality structures based on social demand and specialty characteristics, refine the different categories of majors (or major groups) and talent cultivation requirements for specialties, and avoid blind comparisons and requirement convergence between schools and specialties.

Second, adjust and optimize talent cultivation plans and teaching plans. Newly built undergraduate schools should integrate market demands and the features of professional talent cultivation, and emphasize balanced general knowledge and specialized education, theoretical and practical education, broad and professional ability cultivation, and relationships between demand-based cultivation and laying broad, solid foundations for specialties. They should adjust curriculum systems and update teaching content based on student cultivation objectives and requirements. They should be oriented towards industry and business requirements, improve production-study cooperation and production-education integration, explore diverse talent cultivation models, meet pressing demands by society and the market for applicable, technical talents with strong practical abilities, work hard to improve the concordance of talent cultivation results with social demands, and improve student employment and entrepreneurial abilities.

Third, focus on specialty construction and reform work. Specialties are the platforms and vehicles for talent cultivation, and student quality, cultivation quality, and employment quality are the core indicators for measuring the level of specialty construction, so clear principles of establishing specialties should be defined, specialty establishment should be standardized, specialty structures and connotation should be adjusted, scientific subject systems should be built, and specialty entry, adjustment, and exit mechanisms should be established and improved. The dialectical relationship between specialties and subjects and specialty development and subject building should be properly managed, the fundamental and supporting roles of subject building should be used in specialty development and talent cultivation, and teachers should be guided to use scientific research and technical development to help improve the level of instruction and conditions for cultivation (Zhong 2012b).

Fourth, reform traditional classroom instruction models. Schools should earnestly study new changes in knowledge transmission channels and methods brought by Internet and knowledge digitization technology, focus closely on impacts on talent cultivation work brought by

Internet-based instruction methods such as "massive open online courses," "flipped classrooms," and "micro-lectures," strive to reform traditional class instruction models centered on instructors and teaching materials, explore new education and learning methods such as investigative learning, discussion-based education, and online-offline integrated education, facilitate self-study and cooperative study of students, and emphasize cultivating students' abilities for independent thought, digesting knowledge, recognizing problems, having a critical spirit, and analyzing and solving problems.

Strengthen Human Resource and Material Resource Building

With regards to human resources building, first, improve the instructor team building plan. Newly built undergraduate schools must earnestly study the new features of economic, social, technical, and cultural development, keep up with new trends in international and domestic education reform and development, incorporate the actual situation in the school, and clarify the ideology and key points behind faculty team construction. They must strengthen building teacher morals and academic standards, advocate a spirit of dedication and group work, and focus on career development of teachers. They must optimize faculty team structures, including age, majors, decree, title, and learning origin structures as well as full-time/part-time and "dual profession" teacher structures, and continually improve the overall quality of faculty teams. Next, they must strengthen system building and their policy orientation. They must reform teacher hiring and evaluation systems, guide instructors to improve based on the teacher-learner communication and teaching-research combination, and continually improve their educating and instructional levels. They must emphasize transforming scientific research and technical development resources and results into high-quality teaching resources, transforming them into new content for courses and teaching materials, creating new teaching experiments, and providing graduation thesis (design project) topics for undergraduates, and support the building of specialties with features to create conditions and provide support for cultivating innovative talents. Third, strengthen training work for teachers and management leaders. They must place great emphasis on professional development and on-the-job training for teachers and continually improve the teaching abilities and levels of teachers. They must emphasize cultivation and training work for education managers and student work officials, continually improve the level of school education management and administration of student affairs, and provide human resources support and assurance for improving education quality and student growth. Fourth, be concerned with teachers life and compensation, resolve their family concerns, and work hard to create a good atmosphere for them to have good lives, enjoy work, and grow through competition (Zhong 2012c).

Regarding building materials resources, first, establish a stable expense assurance mechanism. Newly built undergraduate schools should raise school funds through multiple channels, and private higher education institutions with the right conditions should introduce charitable trust mechanisms and foundation systems, and use the legal operation of foundations to raise funds for school development. They should build robust and normalized finance and asset management systems and properly manage funds, while also emphasizing making efficient use of limited funds and resources and properly using funds. Next, strengthen the building of education conditions, including expanding education space, building infrastructures, increasing library resources, updating lab equipment, and building logistics management services and campus IT resources.

Explore Innovations in Internal School Mechanisms

First, newly built undergraduate schools should strengthen systemic research and top-level design for talent cultivation system reforms and internal management system reforms, and actively explore mechanism innovations and learning system innovations. For example, based on demands from economic and social development and school talent cultivation objectives and specifications, perform timely reform explorations of credit systems, short semester systems, and classical academy (school) systems, or attempt diverse reforms such as ordering-list type training and production-learning cooperative education. Next, they must grasp hard-won opportunities for transforming the mode of economic development, scientific and technical development, and college entrance exam and recruiting system reforms, optimize school subject structures, adjust school and department setup and educational organizations, and build an organization framework for deepening overall reforms. They must adapt to the needs of reforms in learning systems and talent management models and explore innovations in education management mechanisms and student affairs administration mechanisms. Third, they must strengthen construction of internal school education quality monitoring and assurance systems, improve quality standards, build robust policy rules, optimize indicator systems, reform evaluation methods, and strengthen evaluation result feedback and improvement mechanisms. They should focus on evaluating student learning results and the effectiveness of resource use, establish student learning result tracking and assessment mechanisms, and continually improve the effectiveness of student learning result and quality assurance systems. Fourth, they must promote and improve the building of modern university systems, formulate and implement university statutes, and provide systemic assurances for deepening talent cultivation model reforms and improving the quality of talent cultivation (Zhong and Zhao 2011).

Create a Good Campus Culture and Education Atmosphere

University culture is the spirit of the university, and the historical accumulation, human character, and value concepts formed by a university through a long course of development. University culture is internalized as a university's education concepts, value pursuits, and academic character, and is externally manifested as a university's institutions, behavioral modes, and material conditions. It silently influences teacher and student thoughts and behaviors and the university's development direction, and is an internal support for improving educational levels and the development of characteristics. Newly built undergraduate schools should place great emphasis on building campus culture, continually optimize their educational atmosphere, and create a good cultural atmosphere for talent cultivation and sustainable development of the school. It should be stressed that campus culture building not only include creating cultural landscapes, sculpts subjects, or displays features, but should also permeates the entire school management and talent cultivation process. They must make full use of the schools' soft resources, use multiple methods such as party building, ideology and politics, student tutorial, advisor systems, and boarding systems to silently influence students in areas such as learning attitude, value concepts, and life objectives. They should strengthen school and learning atmosphere construction and education with a sense of social responsibility, and work hard to form a culture of academic freedom, a culture that appreciates values both the spirit of science and humanities, a culture that integrates the traditional and modern, a diverse culture of tolerant values, and an open culture with a global perspective on campus (Zhong and Zhao 2010).

Finally, it must be pointed out that the data analysis results of the evaluation results show that there is not a significant difference between the pass rate for the main observation points for evaluated schools in the eastern region and evaluated schools in the central and western regions, and some of their failure rates for main observation points were even higher than those in the western region. Comparing the level of regional economic, social, cultural, and education development, this kind of "inversion" phenomenon of the pass rates for main observation points at regional schools contrasts with the general social understanding, and has attracted much attention from eastern authorities of education administration. While supporting some high-level universities to take the lead in development, they must truly strengthen comprehensive support and category-based guidance of newly built undergraduate schools in the region, promote newly built undergraduate schools focusing their efforts on connotation content development and quality promotion work, and better serve regional economic building and social development. On the other hand, regional education administration authorities should highly value and adopt effective measures to strongly support and strictly regulate private universities. Private undergraduate schools should earnestly reflect on their undergraduate education work and adopt targeted measures to make corrections.

ACKNOWLEDGMENTS

This article is a research result of the National Natural Science Foundation Key Project "Research on the Theory of Chinese Education Resource Distribution and Major Practical Issues" (project approval no.: 71133002)

NOTE

1. The original statistical data for this paper came from the Ministry of Education Higher Education Evaluation Center.

REFERENCES

Zhong, B. 2012a. Zhuahao benke jiaoxue hege pinggu, tuozhan youzhi gaodeng jiaoyu ziyuan [Grasping qualification evaluation for undergraduate education, and expanding resources for high-quality higher education]. *Zhongguo gaodeng jiaoyu [China Higher Education]* 19.

Zhong, B. 2012b. Tuijin daxue kejiao ronghe, nuli peiyang chuangxinxing rencai [Promoting university education integration, working to cultivate new-model talents]. *Zhongguo daxue jiaoxue [China University Teaching]* 05.

Zhong, B. 2012c. Gaodu zhongshi gaodeng xuexiao jiaoshi fazhan wenti [Highly valuing the problem of developing higher education institution instructors]. *Zhongguo gaodeng jiaoyu* 18.

Zhong, B. 2013. Rencai peiyang moshi gaige shi gaodeng xuexiao neihan jianshe de hexin [Talent cultivation model reforms are the core of higher education institutions content building]. *Gaodeng jiaoyu yanjiu [Journal of Higher Education]*, vol. 34, no. 1, 11.

Zhong, B., and Y. Zhao. 2010. Jiakuai jianshe Zhongguo tese de daxue wenhua—guanyu dangqian daxue wenhua jianshe gongzuo de ruogan sikao [Hastening construction of university culture with Chinese characteristics—Several thoughts on current university culture building work]. *Guojia jiaoyu xingzheng xueyuan xuebao [Journal of National Academy of Education Administration]* 09.

Zhong, B., and Y. Zhao. 2011. Zhongguo tese xiandai daxue zhidu jianshe—mubiao, tezheng, neirong ji tuijin celüe [Building a modern university system with Chinese characteristics—Objectives, features, content, and promotion strategy]. *Beijing shifan daxue xuebao: shehui kexue ban [Journal of Beijing Normal University, Social Sciences]* 04.

The Value Orientation of Higher Vocational Education Evaluation: A Textual Analysis of an Evaluation Program

Wang Yonglin and Wang Zhanjun

Abstract: Education evaluation should be based on human development and revolve around educational institutions integrating two dimensions, the development needs of the nation and society, and the logic and laws of self-development. The value orientation of higher vocational education evaluation in China is actually expressed through enhancing quality awareness, normalizing education standards, strengthening the central position of teaching, highlighting the characteristics of institutions, changing the focus of the evaluation based on developments in society, and using evaluation concepts in keeping with the times. Due to late start, less experience, and rapid development, there have inevitably been theoretical and practical shortcomings in the evaluation of higher vocational education in China. The value orientation of higher vocational education evaluation should combine instrumental rationality and value rationality, investigate the implicit factors associated with education quality, increase the inherent motivation of institutions to participate in evaluations, promote the separation of governance, management, and evaluation, and conduct normalized, continuous, and dynamic monitoring of teaching quality.

It has been a full decade since the evaluation of higher vocational education began in China in 2004. Its positive effect on developing teaching quality standards and enhancing the quality of talent development in vocational education is undeniable, and it has become an important part of China's higher education quality assurance system. To improve the higher vocational education evaluation program, it has undergone updates and adjustments, but the evaluation work itself has been controversial and subject to continual debate and criticism. Researchers and practitioners must therefore face the important questions of "how to view evaluation and how to conduct evaluations." The value orientation of an education evaluation permeates the entire evaluation process, guides the direction of the evaluation activities, normalizes the behavior of the evaluation subjects, and reflects the core concepts, spirit, and essence of the evaluation

English translation © 2016 Taylor & Francis, LLC, from the Chinese text "Gaodeng zhiye jiaoyu pinggu de jiazhi quxiang yanjiu—Jiyu pinggu fang'an de wenben fenxi" by Wang Yonglin and Wang Zhanjun. Translated by Michelle LeSourd. Originally published in Jiaoyu yanjiu [Educational Research], 2014, vol. 409, no. 2, and funded by China's National Natural Science Foundation Project "Theory and Methods for Higher Education Monitoring and Evaluation" (71273029).

work. The effectiveness of the evaluation work relates directly to whether or not the value orientation is scientific. Researching and reflecting on the value orientation of higher vocational education evaluation from the macro perspective will aid in making timely corrections to biases present in the evaluation, bringing all evaluation functions into full play, and guiding the healthy development of vocational education.

PHILOSOPHICAL ANALYSIS OF VALUE ORIENTATION RATIONALITY OF EDUCATION EVALUATION

Education evaluation is a process, based on the goals of education, that uses valid evaluation techniques and methods to measure, analyze, compare, and provide value judgments on the processes and outcomes of educational activities. Education evaluation performs the functions of guidance, motivation, assessment, diagnosis, adjustment, supervision, and accountability. Its purpose is to ensure basic teaching quality standards and to promote the added value of education and the continual improvement of teaching proficiency. To smoothly achieve the purposes and functions of education evaluation, it is necessary to follow standardized procedures and adhere to a scientific orientation. Otherwise, the evaluation may deviate from its correct focus on the institution's teaching and depart from the basic laws of education. A correct grasp of the value orientation is therefore the most important and fundamental concern of the evaluation work. Whether the value orientation is scientific directly impacts the effectiveness of the evaluation in practice and the direction in which education develops.

Value orientation is an important concept in the domain of value philosophy. When a value subject engages in a value activity, that activity process is directed toward a value objective and reflects the overall tendency and direction of changes in the subject's values. Value orientation is not only the grasp of a concept; it also permeates a series of cognitive and practical activities by people around how to realize their value objectives. Many times it is through practical activities that people embody their value orientation and achieve their value objectives (Ruan 2004). The value orientation will determine the type of practical behavior. Value orientation functions as a social norm, orientation, and driving force (Ruan 2004). It determines a variety of value assessments, value choices, and value creation by social subjects, and provides ideal objectives and norms of behavior for the activities of those subjects. It provides a necessary measure for people's value assessments and value choices; through people's pursuit of their value ideals, it inspires the intrinsic or potential capacity of individuals in a society. The generation of a value orientation is objective; it is subject to the constraints of the mode of production and the social and political systems and ideologies of a given era. Value orientation also has certain subjectivity, because it originates in the needs of the subject and is therefore inevitably colored by subjectivity. To see whether value orientation can play a role in practices, standards, and motivation, we must first examine whether it meets the objective laws of social development, then look at whether its value ideals will be recognized and accepted by society at large.

The fundamental relationship between the internal and external laws of education is a necessary reference for determining the rationality of an evaluation's value orientation.

The internal law of education is that education must be adapted to the physical and mental development of those educated and must promote their self-improvement. The external law of education is that education must be adapted to the political, economic, and social development of a certain era and must meet social demand. Correspondingly, over the course of human education development, education values centering on the individuals have arisen to meet the needs of individual development, and education values centering on society have arisen to meet social demand. Both values have opposed or alternated with each other in different countries and at different times. In this regard, Prof. Pan Maoyuan proposed that the application of the internal law of education must be constrained by the external law, while the external law must be achieved through the internal law. The two should be well integrated when managing education. Accordingly, education values should also integrate meeting both social needs and people's needs for self-development (Pan 1988). With regard to the fundamental relationship between the conflicting internal and external factors, fully exercising the social function of education can only be realized by upgrading the overall quality of individual persons, an internal factor. Integrating individually based and socially based education values must therefore be based on the foundation of human development.

Given the above, a scientific and rational value orientation for education evaluation should guide institutions to coordinate the two dimensions of serving the development needs of the country and society while adhering to the logic and laws of self-development. It should encourage institutions to focus on the long-term benefits of human and social development, uphold intrinsic academic boundaries, and foster the social function of education while breaking down the barriers of short-term, parochial interests. It must to a certain extent rise above social realities in the process of talent development and adhere to educational ideals and long-term goals.

INVESTIGATING THE ACTUAL VALUE ORIENTATION OF HIGHER VOCATIONAL EDUCATION EVALUATION

Education policy is an expression of certain interests and value demands of a policy-making body; it is the medium through which an educational philosophy moves from theory to practice. The value orientation of the higher vocational education evaluation is the basic standpoint and value attitude guiding the evaluation activities, and is an expression of its value inclinations. It permeates the subject's entire practice of evaluation through the vehicle of certain education evaluation policies. Whether explicit or implicit, they normalize the behavior of the evaluation subject, thereby affecting the goals and direction of the evaluation object's activities. The higher vocational education evaluation program is the policy foundation guiding the implementation of the evaluation. Its guiding ideology, system design, indicator system, and evaluation methods all embody the value inclinations of the evaluation subject. It is therefore possible to examine the value orientation of the higher vocational education evaluation using a comparative analysis of documents from China's 2004 Higher Vocational Education Evaluation Program ("old program") and its 2008 Evaluation Program ("new program"). The analysis reveals the following actual expressions of the higher vocational education evaluation's value orientation.

Guiding Institutions to Enhance Quality Awareness, Create Educational Standards, and Improve the Quality Assurance System

Higher vocational education began in China in the early 1980s. As late as 2003, there were only 208 higher vocational institutions in the country. In 2004 the number of such institutions jumped to 1,044 (National Joint Conference of Vocational Institute Presidents 2010), and it reached 1,280 by 2011 (Ministry of Education 2011). Such a leap in the number institutions is rare in the history of higher education in China. The resulting important and urgent task was to normalize quality standards for higher vocational education institutions to enable them to meet the requirements for their level of higher education, while also reflecting the special characteristics of vocational education. The significance of evaluation lies in its judgment, intervention, guidance, and promotion. As an important component of the quality assurance system for higher vocational education and a compass guiding institutions, the primary task of the evaluation was to strengthen administrators' awareness of education quality, standardize the management of vocational institutions, strengthen the quality monitoring of each aspect of talent development work, and promote the improvement of the institutions' internal quality assurance systems.

In 2004, the implementation of the higher vocational education evaluation met in a timely way the objective demand for quality assurance as vocational education expanded rapidly. Internally, the evaluation intervened in the educational activities of higher vocational institutions. The evaluation program and indicator system was used as a vehicle to guide school personnel to follow the laws of talent development, clarify their educational goals, adhere to management standards, strengthen teaching management, increase the construction of basic teaching facilities, and optimize their training models. Implementing school self-evaluations combined with those evaluations conducted by the external experts prompted institutions to reflect on their own teaching and establish internal quality assurance and monitoring mechanisms. It pushed institutions to use the evaluation program as a guide to make timely corrections to those teaching management ideas and behaviors contrary to enhancing teaching quality. Externally, the evaluation led to improvements in the macro-management of higher vocational institutions, gradually developing an education quality assurance system that is school-centered, guided by education authorities, and involves community participation.

Strengthening the Central Position of Teaching; Highlighting the Characteristics of Higher Vocational Education and of Individual Institutions

The function of higher education has continually expanded in recent times, gradually moving into the center of societal life. No matter how close the relationship with the community, however, teaching is recognized as the most important core function of colleges and universities. The basic standard for evaluating higher vocational education institutions was whether they can train "the highly skilled personnel needed on the front lines of production, construction, services, and management." Strengthening the central position of teaching and promoting teaching quality improvement were the starting and ending points of the evaluation. As an important part of Chinese higher education system, the greatest difference between vocational education and general undergraduate education is the applied and technical nature of its training.

The higher vocational education evaluation program was not only designed to reflect the common laws of higher education, but also intended to embody the characteristics of vocational education. "Specialties, curriculum, and practice teaching" are key features shaping talent development and were important components of both the old and new versions of the evaluation program. The new program took the old program's two levels of indicators and upgraded them to main indicators (level-1 indicators) and a greater number of more refined key evaluation points (level-2 indicators), highlighting their importance and underscoring the characteristics of higher vocational education.

Characteristics are an institution's unique stable features, management styles, and development models accumulated and developed over the long term. They are the characteristics and core competitiveness, which differentiate itself from other institutions. Enhancing institutional characteristics aids in reducing the tendency toward homogenization among colleges and universities, and in generating differentiated competition. The two versions of the evaluation program were clear expressions of guidance to higher vocational institutions in highlighting their unique characteristics. In the old program, characteristics or innovation projects were a level-1 indicator for assessment. The new program changed the characteristics indicator to "development of distinctive specialties" (the main indicator), clarified the scope of "distinctive," and elevated distinctive specialties to a more important position.

Shifting the Focus of the Evaluation from Extrinsic to Intrinsic Development to Adapt to Situational Requirements

By comparison, the old program for higher vocational education evaluation focused on extrinsic development, while the new program focused more on intrinsic development. These were clearly expressed in the design of the indicators in the two evaluation programs. For example, the old program focused on assessing school funding, teaching infrastructure, practice teaching conditions, faculty, and other basic assurance conditions. The new program played down the previous physical and quantifiable indicators and paid more attention to intrinsic elements such as the institution's management orientation, teaching management, and teaching quality.

Keeping Evaluation Concepts up with the Times and Continually Improving Its Mechanisms, Methodologies, and Tactics

Since the turn of the twenty-first century, new features have developed in international education evaluation. For example, the focus has changed from cognitive assessment to development and guidance. The evaluation program and indicator system have changed from presupposition to generative, emphasizing joint participation and equal exchange among multiple stakeholders. The evaluation methods have become diversified, modernized, and individualized. To respond to expectations for improvement after the implementation of the first round of evaluation, which exposed problems, the design of the new program actively absorbed the latest concepts in modern education evaluation, and improved the deficiencies of the old program in the following four areas.

First, the program diluted the role of stratification and guided institutions to focus on strengthening their intrinsic development. For example, the new evaluation program was called

"Talent Development Evaluation" instead of "Talent Development Level Evaluation," dropping the word "level." The conclusions of the evaluation were changed from "excellent, good, qualified, or unqualified" to "pass" and "deferred pass," no longer attaching a rating label to the institutions.

Second, changes were made to the orientation of the evaluation tasks. The "quality of the institution's talent development work will be judged, and the evaluation findings will be approved by the educational authorities" under the old program (Ministry of Education 2004) was changed to the "main aspects of the institution's talent development work will be analyzed and assessed, and suggestions and recommendations will be made to improve the work" under the new program (Ministry of Education 2008).

Third, attempts were made to diversify the evaluation subjects to involve vocational education stakeholders in the evaluation process, and to broaden representation in the composition of the expert personnel.

Fourth, the evaluation methods and tools were optimized. The introduction of the Talent Development Data Collection Platform significantly improved the efficiency and validity of the evaluation.

Overall, based on our comparative textual analysis, the differences in value orientation between the two evaluation programs can be summarized in the following four areas. First, in terms of guiding ideology and principles, the old program focused more on extrinsic indicators such as management standards and infrastructure, while the new program emphasized the intrinsic indicators closely related to the quality of education. Second, in terms of the focus, the old program did not sufficiently reflect the characteristics of higher vocational education, while the new program highlighted those characteristics, emphasizing the position of students' practical skills and of community assessment in the evaluation. Third, in terms of the name of the evaluation and its conclusions, the old program emphasized assessing the level of teaching proficiency, while the new program played down stratification and highlighted the evaluation's function to promote the development of teaching work. Fourth, in terms of the mission of the evaluation, the old program made a value judgment based on its conclusions about the teaching, while the new program made recommendations based on its analysis, diagnosis, and improvement of problems with the teaching (Table 1).

Changes in the higher vocational education environment gave rise to the underlying causes of the differences in the value orientation of the two evaluation programs. The old program was formulated during a period of rapid expansion of higher vocational education in China. The primary tasks of the evaluation were to strengthen the infrastructure of institutions, encourage them to standardize their management, enhance their awareness of education quality, promote education and teaching reform, and strengthen institutional macromanagement. The design of the evaluation indicators therefore placed more emphasis on extrinsic development. After 2006, the growth of higher vocational education stabilized, and increasing the quality of education became the focus of attention. Building up quality became the central task of developing higher vocational education. As the situation changed, the shortcomings of the old program became increasingly apparent. As it appeared increasingly less relevant to higher vocational education quality assurance, it became more urgently necessary to improve the program. Based on the previous context, the new program was formulated in line with the concept of soft evaluation rather than hard evaluation, offering a timely response to the requirements of the era and highlighting indicators more closely related to intrinsic development.

TABLE 1
Comparison Table of 2004 and 2008 Higher Vocational Education Evaluation Indicators

2004 level-1 and level-2 indicators	2008 main indicators and key evaluation points
1. Guiding institutional ideology	1. Role of leadership
1.1 School orientation and educational philosophy	1.1 Institution development planning
1.2 Integration of production, study, and research	1.2 Management goals and orientation
	1.3 Degree of emphasis on teaching
	1.4 Stability of campus
2. Faculty development	2. Faculty
2.1 Composition	2.1 Full-time faculty
2.2 Quality and development	2.2 Part-time faculty
3. Teaching conditions and utilization	3. Curriculum development
3.1 Teaching infrastructure	3.1 Curriculum content
3.2 Practice teaching conditions	3.2 Teaching methods
3.3 Teaching budget	3.3 Lead instructors
	3.4 Teaching materials
4. Teaching development and reform	4. Practice teaching
4.1 Specialties	4.1 Teaching internships
4.2 Curriculum	4.2 Practice teaching curriculum system design
4.3 Vocational skills training	4.3 Teaching management
4.4 Quality education	4.4 Practice teaching conditions
	4.5 Double certification
5. Teaching management	5. Development of distinctive specialties
5.1 Management team	5.1 Characteristics
5.2 Quality control	
6. Teaching effectiveness	6. Teaching management
6.1 Knowledge, skills, and character	6.1 Management norms
6.2 Reputation among employers and community	6.2 Student management
	6.3 Quality monitoring
Characteristics or innovation projects	7. Community assessment
	7.1 Student enrollment
	7.2 Employment
	7.3 Social services

IMPROVING THE VALUE ORIENTATION OF HIGHER VOCATIONAL EDUCATION EVALUATION

The past decade of evaluation has been a key period for the development and improvement of higher vocational education in China. The evaluation program was adjusted several times during this period. The concepts, tools, and methods were continually improved, and more than 400 higher vocational institutions underwent the evaluation (Shanghai Academy of Educational Sciences and MyCOS Research Institute 2012). These developments reflected the unremitting efforts of the education authorities and higher vocational educators committed to improving the quality of education. They undoubtedly played a positive role in promoting improved teaching quality and the healthy development of higher vocational education. Nevertheless, the evaluation was a complex and systematic project. The higher vocational education evaluation in China was characterized by a later start, less experience, and rapid expansion. Due to starting later and having less experience, theoretical and practical defects were inevitable in the implementation of the evaluation. We should improve the value orientation of higher vocational education evaluation in the following areas.

Bring Instrumental Rationality and Value Rationality together in Talent Development

Instrumental rationality means an intervention by a subject on an object with the effect of a tool to achieve a certain practical purpose (Wei 2004). It is used to recognize things as they are, to address what kind of relationships people have with the world. Value rationality centers on the subject person; it focuses on the object's significance to the subject and its impact on people's happiness, to reflect the ultimate human value (Xu 2003). Instrumental rationality and value rationality interact and are indivisible. A one-sided emphasis on instrumental rationality will neglect the existence of the person's own values, leading to specific personality distortions or pathological social development in the social environment. The integration of instrumental rationality and value rationality is an inherent requirement for human rationality and the healthy development of society; otherwise, "after we master a powerful tool, without the ultimate value guidance, we will not know what to do with it at a critical time" (Zhai 2002).

Looking at the indicator systems for the old and new higher vocational education evaluation programs, they both expressed a strong instrumental rationalist value orientation in terms of talent development and were colored by utilitarianism. The social function of higher vocational education was overemphasized. The individual functions of self-development and self-existence of students as the subjects of education were severely weakened. Value rationality was not sufficiently reflected in the evaluation, specifically in the areas described subsequently.

First, the needs of external stakeholders—society and employers—became the primary teaching quality evaluation criteria, overlooking the internal stakeholders—students—exploring their own values and concerns. The indicators emphasized that higher vocational education must first obey and serve the needs of national economic construction, social development, and economic modernization. Meeting the societal needs of employers, families, and students became the fundamental basis for the training goals and quality standards. The objectives, curriculum, and specialties had to be adapted to the front-line needs of production, construction, management, and services. Improving employment was the guiding objective for institutions in teaching and curriculum design, building faculty, and developing disciplines and specialties.

Second, highlighting the assessments of external subjects such as community members and employers in evaluating teaching quality overlooked the feelings and experiences of internal subjects like faculty and students. In the old program, assessments by community members were reflected in the level-2 indicator, "Reputation among employers and community." In the new program, community assessment was included as a separate first-level indicator, and its position in the evaluation was elevated. The indicators did not sufficiently include assessment by faculty and students, who are the most closely related to the process of education and teaching.

The presence of value rationality provides spiritual impetus for the existence of instrumental rationality, the presence of which in turn provides support for realizing value rationality. A person's successful realization of objectives and rules in social practice depends on the integration of value rationality and instrumental rationality (Wei 2004). An evaluation is similar to a conductor's baton directing the management of the institution. It should organically integrate the value pursuits of spurring the school to follow the intrinsic laws of education and of meeting the actual needs of society. With regard to value orientation, a scientific and rational evaluation must firmly integrate value rationality and instrumental rationality.

As Eric Ashby said, the strength of government and society and the intrinsic logic and power of higher education institutions mutually restrain each other and jointly determine the direction of the institution. The inherent logic and power of the institution sometimes have a greater impact on it than the power of the government and the society. This inherent logic and power comes from educators' deep convictions and adherence to educational goals that do not always meet society's demands of the higher education system (Ashby 1974). While evaluation guides higher vocational institutions to develop their own characteristics and stay close to the needs of the community, it should also guide them to uphold the intrinsic characteristics of talent development in a complex social environment. When setting training goals, a proper distance should be maintained from social realities, and the focus placed on improving students' individual competencies and comprehensive qualities. Only in this way can we achieve the healthy and sustainable development of higher vocational education.

Design Evaluation Program to Highlight Implicit Factors in the Teaching Process

In the existing evaluation programs, developing faculty, building curricula and specialties, practice teaching, teaching management, and other factors closely related to teaching quality are reflected in the evaluation indicators. These, however, are external, explicit, physical indicators, and can only provide basic assurances for improving education quality; their impact on teaching work will gradually weaken over time. Under the conductor's baton of the evaluation, even if higher vocational institutions meet or exceed the requirements for these indicators, it may not necessarily result in a significant improvement in teaching quality. It is the implicit factors that genuinely play a key role in enhancing teaching quality, but they are difficult to measure or grasp through quantitative or intuitive methods; they include education philosophy, teaching models, teaching methods, education environment, and innovative spirit. The existing evaluation programs have played a positive role in spurring the improvement of explicit teaching conditions, but the program design has failed to fully reflect the implicit factors described above. Higher vocational institutions' usual teaching concepts, models, and methods have not yet to be substantially improved. Lip service has been paid to being people-centered and innovations in teaching, but the evaluation work has not yet to touch the core of teaching. In addition, the existing evaluation programs are in essence institution-wide evaluations to examine the overall situation at the school; they have not yet to go deeper into specific disciplines and specialties, schools and departments, and curricula. To this end, future higher vocational education evaluations should use innovative evaluation formats and methods to develop a discipline and specialty accreditation and evaluation system, and should examine the implicit factors in the teaching process to achieve a genuinely in-depth evaluation of teaching.

Increase the Inherent Motivation of Institutions to Participate in the Evaluation

Optimizing the impact of the higher vocational education evaluation will only be achieved by increasing the enthusiasm and inherent motivation of institutions to participate in the evaluation.

At present, the higher vocational education evaluation in China is implemented using a top-down approach initiated by the government. Basic questions such as timing, format, and schedule are determined by the government; it is a government-led, external administrative activity. In essence, the evaluation not only assesses talent development at higher vocational institutions, but also implies educational accountability. In this context, the underlying assumptions of the evaluation are based on "no confidence" in the evaluated entity; the evaluation becomes a kind of "punishment" for that entity. Under the existing model, the passive participation of higher vocational institutions in the evaluation consists of completing "certain tasks" for their superiors. They focus on the ability to "make a good report" and "get through successfully" rather than on making tangible improvements addressing the urgent quality needs of their own institution. It therefore appears that evaluation is simply a burden for many institutions. They lack the inherent motivation to participate and it is difficult to mobilize the enthusiasm of faculty and students. The evaluation process is prone to institutions simply playing along or even committing fraud, ultimately leading to a great reduction in the practical effect of the evaluation.

In this regard, we can try establishing an evaluation system in which institutions apply for accreditation on their own initiative. Based on the results of their self-evaluation, they would voluntarily determine whether to participate and at what rating level. It would be implemented in the following manner: The education authorities authorize the establishment of an intermediary accreditation entity to develop evaluation criteria for different accreditation standards (e.g., a qualifying certification, an outstanding certification, and so on). Institutions carry out a self-assessment to determine whether to participate in the accreditation and at which level to apply. The accreditation entity implements evaluations of the institutions based on the level and type of their applications, provides feedback and suggests improvements to the institutions, and consults with them in determining the accreditation results. The institutional accreditation evaluation results are released to the public and the valid period of the accreditation is specified. Such an evaluation model will move institutions from "they are making us participate" into "we want to participate." It will make internal demand the starting point for higher vocational institutions and increase their initiative and enthusiasm for being part of the evaluation.

Promote the Separation of Governance, Management, and Evaluation in the Evaluation System

Currently, the Chinese education management and evaluation system is characterized by a concentration of the three functions of governance, management, and evaluation within the hand of the government. The government sets the rules of the game, implements the rules, and makes judgments based on those rules. Such a government-led evaluation system results in at least the following three drawbacks.

First, it makes the diversification of evaluation subjects a mere formality. Although the new higher vocational education evaluation program specifically involves students, the community, employers, and other diverse stakeholders, since the government-led pattern has not changed, the evaluation process has a strong administrative flavor. Those stakeholders' level of participation and right to speak is far from sufficient, and they cannot play their expected roles.

Second, it effects the objectivity and scientific nature of the evaluation findings. Education authorities in some regions, due to a variety of interest considerations, do not make stringent enough inspections of the evaluation findings. Some even use the findings of expert groups to raise evaluation ratings, contaminating those findings with additional human factors and administrative bias.

Third, it limits the function of intermediary evaluation agencies. During the reform process that has transformed government functions and the education management system, some professional education evaluation agencies came into being and play a role in various types of evaluations. Due to institutional constraints, however, such agencies still lack a sufficiently independent position in society and a smooth relationship with government and the community. Their role in the evaluation process therefore remains very limited.

Promoting the separation of governance, management, and evaluation should be the goal of future higher vocational education evaluation system reforms in China. The purpose of such a separation is to rebuild the relationship between the government, higher education institutions, evaluation agencies, and society. Its essence is to balance authorities and interests, and the key lies in the government's decentralization, functional transformation, and separation of government undertakings. After such a separation, the role of government in education evaluation will be macromanagement and coordination, regulatory guidance, developing standards, and supervision and monitoring. It will appropriately delegate evaluation authority to the intermediary agencies, rather than intervene excessively in evaluations. Higher vocational institutions must establish and improve their self-evaluation and quality assurance systems, while actively participating in and accepting evaluation and accreditation by external evaluation agencies and industry accreditation organizations. The intermediaries should be established as independent legal entities under the national legal framework, with clearly defined responsibilities and a clear relationship with the government. They should also upgrade their standards for evaluation work to ensure its quality, and take the initiative to provide institutions and the community with professional evaluation and consulting services.

Make Education Quality Monitoring Normal, Continuous, and Dynamic

Both existing higher vocational education evaluation programs have two characteristics in terms of format: First, the evaluation measures, judges, and assesses educational outcomes already determined; it examines the effectiveness of the outcomes and overlooks the process factors of education implementation. Second, the implementation cycle is once every certain number of years; it is a one-time, summative evaluation with a longer interval. Such a format is deficient in three areas: One, there is an information feedback lag; nothing can be done about activities already completed. Biases and flaws in the education process can only begin to be diagnosed in the next evaluation cycle. Two, the conclusions and recommendations can only provide information and assistance for future improvements, but no early warning, intervention, or correction can be made for the presence of biases in educational activities currently being implemented. Three, the evaluation findings can only statically reflect the outcomes of educational activities and cannot dynamically reflect the education process.

Government education documents have specified that making higher vocational education quality monitoring more normal, continuous, and dynamic is the future direction for improving education evaluation. For example, the word "monitoring" appears nine times in the National Education Plan 2010–20, which proposes to "improve the monitoring and evaluation system and regularly publish monitoring and evaluation reports." Monitoring is based on predetermined educational goals and plans, and is a process of ongoing collection, dynamic tracking, objective description, and timely feedback on the status of various activities, measures, environments, resources, and other process factors affecting education and teaching. It provides a systemic examination and evaluation of the impact of such process factors on education outcomes. After collecting and tracking information on the education implementation process, judgments can be made about whether education activities and behavior are implemented according to the predetermined plan and about their progress toward the intended educational goals (Creed 2003; Tibaijuka 2003). Compared with traditional evaluation, monitoring is more concerned about the process of talent development. It aims to find out the reasons for the successes and failures of educational activities, to improve the implementation and decision making of educational programs, increase the efficient use of educational resources, enhance the transparency of public information on the quality of education, and implement accountability in education. Monitoring is fundamentally continuous, systematic, timely, and provide feedback; compared to traditional evaluation, monitoring places a more thorough, comprehensive, and systematic focus on education quality.

REFERENCES

Ashby, E. 1974. *Adapting universities to a technological society*. San Francisco, CA: Jossey-Bass.

Creed, C. 2003. Program evaluation and its role in quality assurance. *Practitioner Research and Evaluation Skills Training in Open and Distance Learning Handbook* B4:19–21.

Ministry of Education. 2004. Gaozhi gaozhuan yuanxiao rencai peiyang gongzuo shuiping pinggu fang'an [Higher vocational and technical institutions talent development level evaluation program (trial implementation)]. Accessed at http://www.moe.edu.cn/publicfiles/business/htmlfiles/moe/moe_42/201010/110099.html.

———. 2008. Gaodeng zhiye yuanxiao rencai peiyang gongzuo pinggu fang'an [Higher vocational institutions talent development evaluation program]. Accessed at http://www.moe.gov.cn/publicfiles/business/htmlfiles/moe/s3878/201010/110098.html.

———. 2011. 2011 nian tongji shuju [2011 education statistical data]. Accessed at http://www.moe.gov.cn/publicfiles/business/htmlfiles/moe/s7382/201305/152554.html.

National Joint Conference of Vocational Institute Presidents. 2010. *Gaodeng zhiye jiaoyu gaige yu fazhan baogao (2000–2010) [Higher vocational education reform and development report (2000–2010)]*, 28. Beijing: Higher Education Press.

Pan, M. Y. 1988. Jiaoyu de jiben guilu jiqi xianghu guanxi [The fundamental laws of education and their interrelationship]. *Gaodeng jiaoyu yanjiu [Journal of Higher Education Research]* 3, pp. 1–7.

Ruan, Q. 2004. *Jiazhi zhexue [Value philosophy]*, 160, 162. Beijing: Central Party School Press.

Shanghai Academy of Educational Sciences and MyCOS Research Institute. 2012. 2012 Zhongguo gaodeng zhiye jiaoyu rencai peiyang zhiliang niandu baogao [2012 Annual report on the quality of talent development in Chinese higher vocational education]. *Zhongguo jiaoyu bao [China Education Daily]*, 2012-10-17.

Tibaijuka, A. K. 2003. *Monitoring and evaluation guide*, 11–15. Nairobi: UN-HABITAT.

Wei, X. L. 2004. Lun jiazhi lixing yu gongju lixing [On value rationality and instrumental rationality]. *Jiangxi Xingzheng Xueyuan xuebao [Journal of Jiangxi Administration Institute]* 4, pp. 63–67.

Xu, G. Q. 2003. Lun jiazhi lixing [On value rationality]. *Nanjing Shifan Daxue xuebao (shehui kexue ban) [Journal of Nanjing Normal University (Social Science Edition)]* 9, pp. 10–14.

Zhai, Z. M. 2002. Jiazhi lixing de huifu [The resurgence of value rationality]. *Zhexue yanjiu [Philosophical Research]* 5, pp. 15–21.

The Operation Mechanisms of External Quality Assurance Frameworks of Foreign Higher Education and Implications for Graduate Education

Lin Mengquan, Chang Kai, and Gong Le

Abstract: The higher education quality evaluation and assurance frameworks and their operating mechanisms of countries such as the United Kingdom, France, and the United States show that higher education systems, traditional culture, and social background all impact quality assurance operating mechanisms. A model analysis of these higher education quality assurance frameworks shows that quality assurance entities having clear and harmonious responsibilities and interest relations is a precondition to the good operation of higher education quality assurance mechanisms, and the model of internal self-discipline of the higher education institutions taking precedence and internal and external assurances integrating organically is a developing trend in higher education quality assurance.

The construction and development of European and American higher education quality assurance frameworks has a long history. After undergoing a series of changes, they have gradually formed an operating mechanism that has harmoniously developed to suit to national education systems and cultural and social backgrounds. In recent years, with the lively development of international exchanges and cooperation for Chinese higher education and graduate education, even though the academic world has performed a large number of studies and explorations of European and American higher education systems and quality assurance frameworks, they have mostly tended to be practical studies and introductions, and there have not been many discussions of quality assurance operating mechanisms and rules. On the basis of going through foreign quality assurance frameworks, this article focuses on analyzing the cultural and social backgrounds of quality assurance frameworks, comes up with an abstract model of a quality assurance operating mechanism with their common characteristics, and proposes the concept of "degree of harmony" of quality assurance operating mechanisms.

English translation © 2016 Taylor & Francis, Inc., from the Chinese text "Guowai gaodeng jiaoyu waibu zhiliang baozhang kuangjia de yunxing jizhi jiqi dui yanjiusheng jiaoyu de qishi" by Lin Mengquan, Chang Kai, and Gong Le. Translated by Jeff Keller. Originally published in *Gaodeng jiaoyu yanjiu* [Journal of Higher Education], 2010, vol. 31, no. 10, and funded by the Chinese Society of Academic Degrees and Graduate Education Level-One Project (2010W08).
Color versions of one or more figures in the article can be found online at www.tandfonline.com/mced.

As most countries include graduate education in higher education, while discussing foreign graduate education quality assurance frameworks, this article will focus more on higher education overall and mostly discuss its external systems and mechanisms in the hope of drawing lessons for establishing a graduate education external quality assurance framework and operating mechanism in China.

HIGHER EDUCATION QUALITY ASSURANCE FRAMEWORKS IN THE UNITED STATES, THE UNITED KINGDOM, AND FRANCE

In recent years, the size of higher education has expanded, international competition has intensified, and quality assurance has become a hot topic in higher education management system reforms in every country. To a certain extent, education systems determine the basic framework of the national quality assurance system, and as higher education in every country underwent historical changes, quality assurance frameworks with various characteristics were formed. Looking at higher education quality assurance frameworks, those of the United Kingdom, France, and the United States are representative. Discussing the characteristics of these countries' quality assurance frameworks is the basis for recognizing the operating rules of quality assurance. Within quality assurance frameworks, which organizations form and how they form quality assurance entity systems is key to studying the responsibility and interest relations of various institutions in the entity systems.

Higher Education Quality Assurance Framework in the United Kingdom

The British higher education system has continuously adapted to social changes, and in the past few decades, its central authorities, local authorities, governments, and agencies have gradually formed a "diverse cogovernance" model. Assurance entities include both governments and government-appointed or authorized agencies. The diverse cogovernance model has allowed stakeholders to achieve mutual checks and balances in power distribution and operation. Under the diverse cogovernance model, the tradition of higher education institution (HEI) self-discipline has exhibited a state of stable operations in the mutual divergence and systematic integration of administrative and academic power (Liu 2006).

Entity System

The United Kingdom is a typical representative of the "part-official, part-private quality assurance institution model." The British quality assurance entity system is mainly made up of the Quality Assurance Agency for Higher Education (QAA) and also includes the UK higher education funding bodies and the Research Excellence Framework (REF). The British higher education external quality assurance framework has gradually undergone a process of moving from dispersion to unification and from emphasizing external quality assurances to establishing effective internal quality assurances. External evaluations are mainly funded by the UK higher education funding bodies. The QAA and REF are appointed to respectively make academic and research evaluations of HEIs. The academic evaluations are further divided into subject evaluations and HEI evaluations. The QAA, established in 1997, is fully responsible for matters of assuring the quality of British higher education, and it provides fair, objective, and accurate evaluation conclusions to the government and public. The focus of the reviews is not to directly evaluate the educational quality of HEIs, but rather to evaluate the effectiveness of internal HEI quality assurance frameworks.

Responsibilities and Interests

Within the entity system, QAA is an independent body for evaluating higher education that is mainly responsible for auditing HEIs' work on educational quality assurance mechanisms and the academic quality of the courses, while the UK higher education funding bodies are responsible for evaluating the research quality of HEIs. The specific duties of the QAA are: cooperating with higher education funding bodies, teachers, students, and employers, safeguarding the interests of students and public, and safeguarding academic standards and the quality of higher education. They also provide students and employers with information on academic standards and higher education quality to help them in decision making and gaining an understanding, and also support public policy making. They improve the management and guarantee of higher education standards and quality, and facilitate a broader understanding by the public of the nature of higher education standards and quality, including the understanding of related reference standards and the understanding of conventions in European countries and around the world (QAA 2010). Nongovernment personnel are in charge of the QAA's quality assurance work, and the government is only responsible for formulating overall scientific research policies and controlling the overall amount of appropriations and not interfering in concrete work. Therefore, through quality assurance intermediary institutions such as the QAA, the British government has realized indirect intervention and control over higher education.

Higher Education Quality Assurance Framework in France

The French government attaches great importance to education, and education expenses have been at the top of their financial budget for a long time, accounting for approximately 23%, which is first in the world. France's public education system is in an absolutely leading position, and the huge education expenditures guarantee that the state assumes the education expenses for all public HEIs. All public school students are offered free education and can also obtain government benefits for food, transportation, and health insurance. Investors often have the right to guide management, and with huge education investments, the French government has a guiding position in managing education. Its higher education quality assurance is also characterized by centralized supervision, and all evaluations and management is comprehensively planned and controlled by the government.

Entity System

France is a typical representative of "the model of state-control independent from educational administration unit quality assurance institutions." Led by the Comité national d'evaluation (CNE), along with institutions such as the Committee on Evaluating Universities (CEU), National Council for Higher Education and Research (CNESER), and Commission Engineer Titles (CTI), they make up the main framework for French quality assurance. France's higher education evaluation institution is the CNE, which is an independent administrative entity that on the one hand is independent of the government and directly reports to the president, and on the other hand it is independent from the evaluated HEIs and is not led by the minister of education. Apart from CNE, the main French institutions that participate in external higher education evaluation also include: CEU, which is mainly responsible for teacher recruitment and evaluation; CNESER, which is responsible for approving education programs that want to develop to obtain national degree accreditation; CTI, which is mainly responsible for engineering research evaluation and plays a certain kind of indirect responsibility role; the Degree Granting Committee, which falls under the Ministry of Education Higher Education Council, authorizes graduate courses and grants the corresponding degrees; the University Council, which has the functions of formulating academic plans, determining national levels and supplementing and facilitating academic personnel development for all universities; and the National Committee for Science, Technology, and Education, which is a key institution that determines four-year research contracts and distributes Ministry of Education research funds (Xu and Li 2008).

Responsibilities and Interests

CNE's main responsibilities are evaluating French public HEIs, including universities and HEIs governed by the Ministry of Higher Education and HEIs governed by other government authorities, and understands and judges the results of their contract performance. It also researches major issues in higher education and how to improve HEI management and the effectiveness and quantity of higher education and scientific research. It conducts follow-up evaluations of evaluated HEIs to examine the impact of the evaluations on HEI management functions. This work is often conducted around 18 months after issuance of the final evaluation report. CNE's evaluation contents involve all fields related to the mission of public higher education authorities, such as pre-employment and postemployment education, student living conditions, scientific research and use of its findings, methods of managing HEIs, and HEI policies. However, it does not have the power to evaluate individuals and is not authorized to approve courses or distribute state funds. CNE is funded from state finances and possesses complete power of self-governance. Its evaluation activities are aimed at strengthening the self-governance of HEIs and increasing their responsibilities. It separates higher education evaluators and managers, guaranteeing the objective and fair nature of its higher education evaluations, and also guaranteeing that evaluation committees and their personnel have considerable status and authority, so the evaluation results are comparably scientific in nature. Through the president's direct responsibility, appropriations, and right to appoint evaluation committee members, the state plays a macrocontrol, coordinating, and supervising role in CNE's evaluations and operations (National Evaluation Commission 2010).

Higher Education Quality Assurance Framework in the United States

When the United States was founded, its constitution stipulated that the federal government did not have the right to interfere in education in the states. After the Civil War ended in 1865, the United States started feeling the necessity of establishing a central institution to lead education. In 1868, the Department of the Interior added an Education Office, but its duties were limited to managing a small federal education fund and providing help and consultation to HEIs in the states. The federal government did not officially establish the Ministry of Education until 1979. State, regional, and local boards of education still control the real power in their respective education policies, development and planning, and fund allocation. With the continual increase in education expenses and passage of several education laws such as the National Defense Education Act, Education for All Handicapped Children Act (targeted toward education of gifted children), and Adult Education Act, the education policies of the central government gradually penetrated into the states. Since education is targeted at everyone, and involves the future of all families and individuals, in the United States, education is both a major national issue and also a major issue for state and local governments and social groups. Therefore, the greatest feature of the American education system is that government and social forces invest a lot of manpower, materials, and finances in education, forming a multitrack education system, mobilizing the initiatives of diverse forces to run schools, and applying market rules for education with "three comprehensives" (covering all people, all aspects, and the entire course). Compared to education that purely relies on government investment (single-track system), the multitrack education system has greater efficiency and better results. In terms of education quality assurance, the United States is characterized by the model of dominating agencies. The assurance entities in this model are agencies linking governments and HEIs, and the agencies have cooperative and mutually complimentary relations with the state and federal governments in the quality assurance framework.

Entity System

The United States is a typical representative of the "private quality assurance agency model." American private schools, professional evaluation and accreditation organizations, and the Council for Higher Education Accreditation (CHEA) that has a coordinating and managing function constitute the quality assurance entity system. American evaluation and accreditation agencies are generally private organizations independently formed from HEIs and professional associations, and based on differences in their evaluation targets they can be divided into HEI accreditation organizations and professional accreditation organizations. There are currently 11 national school accreditation organizations, eight local HEI accreditation organizations, and 61 professional evaluation and accreditation organizations among all American higher education evaluation and accreditation organizations. These organizations receive government funding and are also independent of the government and are higher education evaluation and accreditation agencies, established under the law and characterized with many forms (Shen and Zhang 2008). CHEA coordinates and recognizes of the accreditation operations and credibility of these organizations.

Responsibilities and Interests

With regards to organizational structure, American intermediary accreditation organizations are agencies with a membership system formed by higher education associations, HEIs, and various social representatives and organizations with willing participants. American higher education evaluation is a voluntary activity on the part of HEIs. American higher education evaluation and accreditation organizations are an integral part of this volunteer system. This voluntariness is mainly manifested as: first, American higher education evaluation organizations are formed by voluntary unions of various schools. This is the case for the New England Association of Schools and Colleges, New England Secondary School Consortium, and higher education accreditation organizations in other regions of the United States Second, HEIs or relevant schools willingly apply to participate in the evaluation activities of these organizations, and without submitting an application, the accreditation organization will not actively evaluate them, nor do they have the right to enforce participation in accreditation. The responsibilities and rights of accreditation institutions and educational institutions are coordinated by willingly established organizations and not through enforcement. The responsibilities of accreditation agencies are communicated between HEIs and HEIs, HEIs and society, and HEIs and professional industries through accreditation activities. However, accreditation agencies directly impact the reputation, sources of students, and financial assistance for HEIs through the results of accreditation, and most HEIs in the United States can actively participate in accreditation, so these types of agencies have strong social influence. The U.S. federal government Ministry of Education and state government education authorities have no legally granted power to manage the evaluation agencies, and they are partners who are treated equally and respect one another, and do not have a manager-managed relationship.

To sum up, in all of the countries, the quality assurance entity systems are made up of several quality evaluation and assurance institutions on different levels or with different natures, and the relevant agencies in the entity system complete the country's different demands for quality evaluation and assurance. Within the higher education systems of different countries, the responsibilities and interest relationships of these agencies, governments, and educational units have different characteristics, and the responsibilities and interests of each party within the assurance entity system are important factors determining the harmonious operation of the quality assurance mechanism.

THE BACKGROUND AND OPERATING RULES OF FOREIGN HIGHER EDUCATION EXTERNAL QUALITY ASSURANCE FRAMEWORKS

Apart from the influence of the previous quality assurance entity systems and responsibility and interest relations, their historical, cultural, economic and social backgrounds have an important impact on the concepts and operating mechanisms of higher education quality assurance.

Cultural Background and Concepts of Quality Assurance

Cultural traditions have broad and deep influence on higher education, and while influencing understandings of quality, they also influence understandings of quality assurance responsibilities. Analyzing the role and impact of cultural background in quality assurance mechanisms can help us more deeply understand the internal causes of the creation and harmonious development of foreign quality assurance mechanisms.

Liberalism and conservatism are the ideological foundations of Western values. Liberal values have formed notions of academic independence and quality self-assurance and a tradition of focus on internal quality assurance, and ideology of conflicting with interference from external evaluations. Since the establishment of higher education quality assurance systems in the United Kingdom and France, conservatism has brought them a state of relatively stable development, and their changes are characterized by their incremental nature. The relatively stable quality assurance frameworks in the United Kingdom and France are supported by conservative thought (Li 2008).

Individualism and pragmatism are more prominent in the United States Individualism has formed value pursuits with the objective of individual interests and development, and reveres individual efforts. Pragmatism is also an educational value with a dominant position in the United States, and cultivating applicable talents with "independent spirits" and "innovative mentalities" is a goal of higher education there. Under this kind of ideological domination, curriculum setup in American higher education has a clear pragmatic and professional nature. Concepts of higher education quality assurance particularly stress evaluation and accreditation of specialties and curriculums (Li and Lü 2009).

A principle of fairness is also reflected in people in these countries through limiting value pursuits and adjusting the relations between individuals, between individuals and governments, and between sovereign nations to achieve a state of harmony and order and gradually form a culture of credibility, which thereby generates academic credibility that plays a similarly active role in the education quality management system.

Social Background and Focus of Quality Assurance

The basic function of higher education is to serve economic, scientific, and social development, and education objectives, and the quality assurance frameworks and assurance emphases, which are established based on the education objectives change with social change and changing demands for economic and scientific development.

During the second half of the twentieth century, the demand from great development of higher education in France, expansion in size of higher education, economic growth, and industrial adjustment required that higher education be centered on "quality" and based on a quality assurance framework. In 1968, 1984, 1989, and 1998, France respectively carried out four rounds of higher education legislation and reforms to suit the changing needs of society and the focus of its quality assurance also changed. Currently the key focus of evaluation assurance in France led by CNE is the state of HEIs on the whole and academic subjects (Yang and Liao 2006).

In the 1990s, subject evaluation was fiercely attacked by HEIs in the United Kingdom, and coupled with tight expenses, the United Kingdom had to improve quality, encourage competition among institutions, improve schooling benefits, and strongly demand a decrease in the overall cost of quality evaluation and assurance. Therefore, in 2002 the QAA started improving the evaluation and assurance framework with a focus on evaluating the effectiveness of internal quality assurance systems of educational institutions and having educational institutions be responsible themselves for specific quality assurance processes and methods.

External Quality Assurance Mechanisms and Operating Rules

The harmonious operation of quality assurance systems is the objective sought by all countries, and the "degree of harmony" shows the extent of harmony in the operations of assurance mechanisms and extent of stability and effectiveness in the systems.

1. Assurance framework model. On the basis of reviewing and analyzing British, American, and French higher education quality assurance systems, we came up with an abstract general framework of quality assurance, or a "systemic framework" (see Figure 1). The model depicts higher education quality assurance entity systems and the relations between them. A model can more directly reflect the quality assurance frameworks of representative countries and helps to effectively analyze the principles, stability, and ability for sustained development of assurance system operation.

   The figure includes the basic structure of the assurance system model, and the model is made up of internal and relevant external institutions of educational institutions. In most countries the stakeholders in the assurance system are mainly external assurance agencies such as the governments, authoritative professional assurance

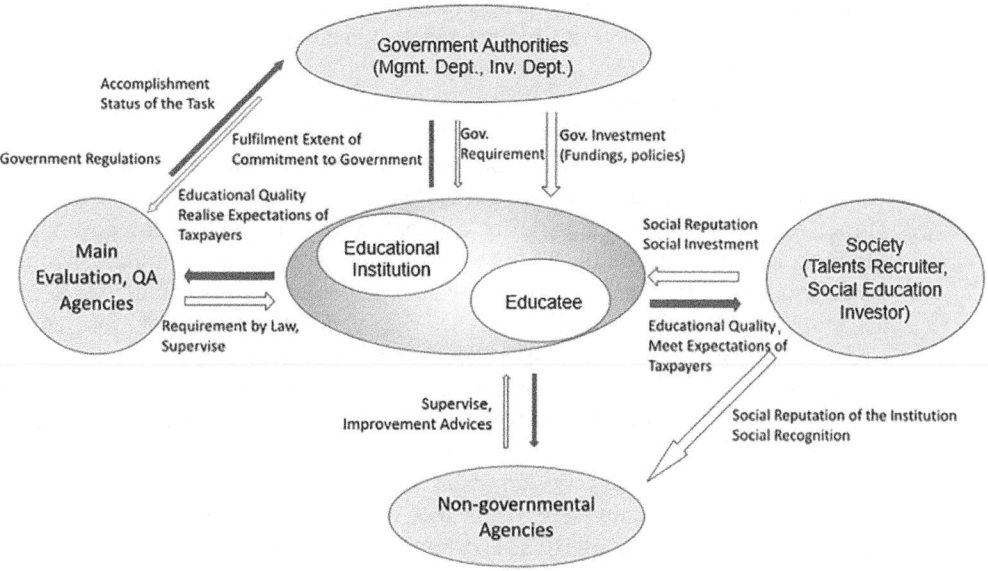

FIGURE 1 Higher education quality assurance framework model.

institutions, and nongovernment agencies, and educators and education recipients. The arrows between stakeholders in the figure represent the relations of responsible and interested parties for quality assurance.

2. Assurance framework model operating rules. The relationships between the entities in the assurance framework model reflect the state of the assurance framework. The relations between one entity and another in the model determine whether the assurance system model operates well and reflects the degree of harmony of its operation. If the relationship between educational institutions and society is the following: educational institutions provide society with high-quality education and cultivates students who meet the practical needs of society, they can obtain social recognition and good social reputations, thereby recruiting more high-quality students, raising tuition fee collection standards, and obtaining government support. If nongovernment professional evaluation organizations independently carry out university and subject ranking activities and indirectly supervise educational institutions, educational institutions that provide high-quality education will have good rankings and similarly obtain high social reputation and recognition from students and parents.

3. Analysis of the degree of harmony of British assurance framework model operations. The British model is divided into the two main modules of internal and external parts, and its previous assurance system operations were not harmonious enough. As mentioned previously, there were severely inharmonious relationships in the pervious British quality assurance framework. The main problems: the first was that with government education funding shrinking, they hoped to assure quality by increasing education efficiency, and thus they issued higher education white papers, organized and formulated education standards, and required or recommended evaluations under a uniform review system; the second was that the "Continuing and Higher Education Act" required that higher education funding councils perform "in-depth education evaluations" of the HEIs they invested in, including evaluations of subjects and HEIs from before the founding of QAA in 1997, which took up a lot of manpower and finances, and the results lacked reliability. Therefore, QAA was criticized on all sides (Jin 2005). The cause was that evaluations were too specific, and greatly increased the burden on schools and cost of education management, which departed from the core values of British academic culture and cultural background of liberalism and conservatism. Misplaced responsibilities interests for external institutions such as the government and QAA and HEIs caused major disharmony in the assurance system. After reforms, the current British assurance system has relatively harmonious operations. There were major reforms to British quality assurance measures after 2002, and "Institutional Audits" issued by QAA was the main measure of external quality supervision. First, looking at the responsibility and interest relationships among governments and other entities, the British government acted based on the fundamental needs of the nation for higher education, upheld taxpayer interests, and legislated authority for QAA to perform external quality supervision of institutions based on the Institutional Audit standards, and these quality supervision focus only on the effectiveness of internal quality assurance systems of HEIs, and provided HEIs with beneficial advice. The responsibility for designing specific quality standards and how to meet these standards through management lay with the HEIs themselves. Second, looking at the

responsibility and interest relations between QAA and education agencies, evaluations from external institutions such as QAA are not forced on HEIs. In this supervisory model HEIs have the right of self-determination, follow education rules, perform quality management under the macroleadership of QAA, and improve the quality of student cultivation. As the external investigations of QAA did not disturb HEIs very much and schools had low costs and good efficiency for the undergoing inspections, this kind of inspection method was widely welcomed. The responsibility and interest relations between HEIs and main external assurance agencies were scientific and harmonious. Third, looking at responsibility and interest relationships between external agencies, the QAA's methods have been recognized by society, students, and employers, and investing institutions such as foundations are willing to invest in education. The government does not impose specific methods on QAA inspections, and gives special agencies enough space. When QAA formulates inspection methods, it fully communicates with universities and conforms to the interests of multiple parties. In the end QAA completed its government-appointed task of protecting "core academic values and the interests of students and society" well. We can see that within the current British quality assurance framework, the scientific and reasonable responsibility and interest relations between all sides has made the operations of assurance systems have greater harmony compared to that before 2002.

The situation in France and the United States can also be analyzed using the above model. For example, the United States completely realizes self-discipline based on united organizations in the education sector itself, and professional united organizations such as ABET and AACSB have participants from education and industry. CHEA, a united association organization, also regulates the self-discipline institutions and is responsible toward society. These responsibility and interest relations have American characteristics, and the self-discipline behavior of accreditation agencies is appreciated by society. If government and social investment organizations recognize the accreditation results of these agencies toward higher education, they will have confidence in investing in higher education.

Of course, in pursuit of a more beautiful, more harmonious education environment, in the face of new challenges, the countries spared no effort to use measures to reform quality assurance and responsibility and interest relations between assurance entities to facilitate the good operations of assurance systems and improve the quality of higher education. For example, the United States faces common problems in accreditation of HEIs and professional education quality: there are no direct exchanges between the governments and universities, so should the governments remain "hands-off" in supervision of higher education quality? In recent years there has been much pressure on the federal government from itself and society, because the assurance of education quality will affect problems like employment, tuition, and contribution of students toward society. This is a comprehensive social problem, and the government bears the brunt of this kind of pressure. Quality accreditation agencies face government pressure and doubts from the public and HEIs. Therefore, the government has increasingly involved in education, and even used legislation to make requirements for schools and accreditation agencies, for example by controlling government appropriations to restrict HEIs. It has played the role of representing social accountability, suddenly inspected various accreditation committees and spot-checked accredited HEIs, and restricted the behaviors of accreditation agencies.

IMPLICATIONS

As different countries have different political systems, economic systems, and cultural backgrounds, they have different understandings of higher education. Even though there are no absolute advantages or disadvantages in educational systems and quality assurance methods, the cultural backgrounds, social backgrounds, and operating rules of higher education quality assurance systems in countries such as the United Kingdom, France, and United States still have enlightenment for higher education quality assurance system development in China.

Cultural and Social Background and Educational Systems Are Important Factors Affecting the Development of Higher Education Quality Assurance Frameworks

Traditional cultural factors have deep-rooted impacts on the field of education. The values of Western liberalism, conservatism, and pragmatism are reflected prominently in views of higher education quality and they are embodied in British universities not being willing to be subjected to excessive external supervision and the American higher education quality assurance system with the feature of professional accreditation. The same is true for the impact of social development on quality value orientations in higher education. Changes in governance of state culture, science and technology, and economics also has a clear impact on higher education, as it changes the interrelationships between government, society, and HEIs. Since higher education is increasingly important to national development, governments have new connections with HEIs in ways from purely providing universities with education resources to relying on contract, performance, appropriation, evaluation, and market mechanisms, and this requires universities to further increase their quality, effectiveness, and educational vigor. Being responsible to the government and society and guaranteeing quality have become important, integral parts of higher education systemic reforms.

Because it is accustomed to the management model characterized by government guidance and administrative orders, China has a relatively weak foundation for education institution autonomy, lacks internal motivation and consciousness of self-discipline for self-assurance, and lacks the correct understanding of the role of external quality assurance. The experiences of countries and regions around the world show that in building a graduate education quality assurance system with Chinese characteristics, the above factors must be considered first, and while managing the relationship between external and internal quality assurance, in the current stage the external role needs to be more powerful than in the West.

The Model of Relying Primarily on Internal Self-Discipline of HEIs and Integration of Internal and External Assurances Has Become the Consensus in Developing Higher Education Quality Assurance

Assuring and improving quality are the common objectives of higher education participants, and in assurance frameworks centered around quality assurance, education institutions are the entities but not the targets of quality assurance. However, since external and internal entities of education institutions have similar quality assurance functions, the various entities in the quality assurance system models can often be divided into external and internal parts of the education institution, and this makes it easier to sort out the responsibility and interest relationships of the various internal and external entities.

Quality process management established within universities is primarily self-monitoring and is supplemented by evaluations of the effectiveness of internal quality management conducted by external agencies such as evaluation agencies and governments, and this kind of quality assurance scheme has become the consensus in the field of foreign higher education quality assurance. As the status of HEIs has improved, the status of their quality assurance entities has correspondingly improved. Governments and society believe that HEIs should take up the most primary, most direct responsibility for assurance. The quality assurance model of "internal as primary and external as secondary" benefits the formation of a harmonious state of universities upholding their autonomy and academic freedom within reasonable limitation, the government focusing on macromanagement and indirect control, professional assurance agencies serving as bridges between HEIs and the government, and building quality assurance standards and evaluating the effectiveness of assurance mechanisms.

Currently, the basic framework of quality supervision in China consists of the administrative and periodical governmental evaluations as the main line, the self-evaluations of educational institutions as the key, and the active participations of professional assurance agencies and other social organizations. But, to meet the new requirements of the national education reform guidance and form a comprehensive and harmoniously operating quality assurance system, we still must make unremitting efforts. The current state of quality assurance of graduate education in China is still a certain ways off from developing into the more active and autonomous internal quality assurance mechanisms of the HEIs. Therefore, currently external supervision is still in an important position, but the most important objective of external supervision is facilitating the establishment of internal quality assurance mechanisms.

Quality Assurance Entities Having Clear, Harmonious Responsibilities and Interest Relationships Is a Precondition to the Good Operation of Higher Education Quality Assurance Mechanisms

Higher education quality assurance frameworks involve multiple assurance entities, and there must be a clear, reasonable division of the responsibilities and interests of each quality entity to be able to increase the fairness and effectiveness of assurances and cause the harmonious operation of the assurance system. The characteristics of the quality assurance frameworks of each country are actually the different responsibilities and interests of the various entities within the quality assurance frameworks. Interests cannot be understood as a kind of right, as they also include reputation, honors, and achievements, and responsibilities originate from duties bestowed by laws and regulations or from self-restrictions generated by industry self-discipline, professional ethics, and market mechanisms.

As described previously, looking at the internal and external responsibilities and interests in the British higher education assurance system, the external assurance duty of QAA is to be responsible for reviewing education quality guarantee mechanisms and academic quality within HEIs. HEFCE is responsible for evaluating the quality of research, while the government that represents national interests is responsible for formulating scientific research policies and controlling the amount of appropriations. Government controls indirectly involve in formulating scientific research policies and controlling the amount of appropriations. Government controls indirectly involve in higher education institutions through the quality assurance from agencies like QAA. The division between the responsibilities of external and internal assurance institutions has already developed from specific evaluations and supervision of the cultivation process to inspections of the effectiveness of the internal assurance systems of higher education institutions mainly assisted by QAA. The American system of higher education quality assurance with supervision by nongovernment organizations and market mechanisms at its core is facing doubts from society, and the government has started to partially make substantive involvement in agencies and higher education institutions, to balance the disharmony of external and internal quality assurance responsibilities and interests.

Based on the current state of graduate education quality assurance in China, while building a graduate education quality assurance system, we must move past the limitation of inspections and evaluations, and recommend taking action from multiple angles such as authorizations possessed by education institutions for degree awarding and the additional rights of education institutions from these authorizations, their contributions toward cultivation quality, as well as government, professional quality assurance agencies, and society. We must properly manage the responsibility and interest relationships of all parties and facilitate the orderly, highly effective operations of assurance systems.

Internationalization Is a Major Trend in Graduate Education Quality Assurance Building

Under the background of economic globalization, quality assurance is both local and international. To meet the demands of rapidly developing international higher education and cross-border movement of talents, with regards to mutual recognition of international academic degree standards, exchanges and transfers of academic credits, professional accreditation, and information sharing, it is extremely necessary to engage in broad international cooperation and exchange and establish internationally recognized, comparable quality standards and quality assurance systems. Currently, united quality assurance organizations are active on the global and regional level, such as the International Network for Quality Assurance Agencies in Higher Education (INQAAHE), European Association for Quality Assurance in Higher Education (ENQA), and the Asia-Pacific Quality Network (APQN). UNESCO and the Organization for Economic Cooperation and Development jointly formulated "Guidelines on Quality Provision in Cross-Border Higher Education" in 2005, INQAAHE formulated "Guidelines of Good Practice in Quality Assurance" (2007), and ENQA formulated "Standards and Guidelines for Quality Assurance in the European Higher Education Area" (2009) recognized by the European Higher Education Area (EHEA) countries. This shows that higher education quality assurance already has clear features of internationalization and an internationally coordination mechanism has already been formed in developed countries in the European Union. China should actively participate in international higher education quality assurance exchanges and cooperation, reasonably learn from and absorb good methods and experiences, and build an open system of higher education quality assurance. It should actively engage in international exchanges and mutual recognition of quality assurance frameworks, such as the methods of professional industry linkage in the Canberra Accord, and gradually give its own quality assurance standards and system Chinese features while conforming to international development trends, thereby gaining international recognition in this sector.

REFERENCES

Jin, D. 2005. Yingguo gaodeng jiaoyu pinggu yu zhiliang baozhang jizhi: jingyan yu qishi [British higher education evaluation and quality assurance mechanisms: Experiences and lessons]. *Jiaoyu yanjiu [Educational Research]* 1:76–81.

National Evaluation Commission. 2010, September 11. Handbook of standards for quality management in French higher education institutions [EB/OL]. https://www.cne-evaluation.fr/WCNE_pdf/LDRCNE_English.pdf

Li, M. 2008. *Yingguo gaodeng jiaoyu zhiliang baozhang tixi de wenhua fenxi [A cultural analysis of the British higher education quality assurance system].* Wuhan: Wuhan ligong daxue.

Li, M., and G. Lü. 2009. Zhongmei gaodeng jiaoyu zhiliang baozhang jizhi bijiao [A comparison of Chinese and American higher education quality assurance mechanisms]. *Qingdao nongye daxue xuebao (shehui kexue ban) [Journal of Qingdao Agricultural University (Social Sciences)]* 1:73–77.

Liu, L. 2006. Qiantan yingguo de xuewei shouquan shenhe zhidu [A brief discussion of England's academic degree authorization review system]. *Xuewei yu yanjiusheng jiaoyu [Academic Degrees and Graduate Education]* 2:73–76.

QAA. 2010, September 11. An Introduction to QAA. http://www.qaa.ac.uk/aboutus/IntroQAA.pdf

Shen, Y., and X. Zhang. 2008. Ying, Fa, Mei gaodeng jiaoyu pinggu jigou de tedian jiqi qishi [The features and lessons of British, French, and American higher education evaluation institutions]. *Pingjia yu guanli [Evaluation and Management]* 2:22–25.

Xu, F., and H. Li. 2008. Faguo gaodeng jiaoyu zhiliang pinggu jizhi dui woguo de qishi [The French higher education quality evaluation mechanism and lessons for china]. *Jiaoyu tansuo [Education Exploration]* 11:139–40.

Yang, J., and M. Liao. 2006. Faguo gaodeng jiaoyu zhiliang baozhang lifa ji qishi [French higher education quality assurance legislation and lessons]. *Gaojiao luntan [Higher Education Forum]* 1:174–77.

Data-Intensive Evaluation: The Concept, Methods, and Prospects of Higher Education Monitoring Evaluation

Wang Zhanjun, Qiao Weifeng, and Li Jiangbo

Abstract: Higher education monitoring evaluation is a process that uses modern information technology to continually collect and deeply analyze relevant data, visually present the state of higher education, and provide an objective basis for value judgments and scientific decision making by diverse bodies Higher education monitoring evaluation is data-intensive evaluation with the features of intensive temporal scales, diverse spatial scales, and multiple value scales, and its purpose is to serve continual improvements, scientific decision making, and diverse judgments. Monitoring evaluation is a result of applying modern information technology in the field of higher education evaluation and a product of adapting to systemic changes and governance reforms in higher education.

There are two theoretical sources that had a deep impact on the development of higher education evaluation. One was Ralph Tyler's redefinition of education evaluation that began in the 1930s. Another was the theory of quality management that was introduced to the higher education field in the 1980s. In the era of the rapid development of higher education massification, internationalization, and informatization, modern information technology will become the third theoretical source impacting the future development of higher education evaluation. Data-intensive monitoring evaluation is not only a necessary result of the application of modern information technology to the field of higher education, it is also a pressing need in the development and reform of higher education.

STATUS DIMENSIONS: TEMPORAL, SPATIAL, AND VALUE SCALES

I define higher education monitoring evaluation as a comprehensive term: higher education monitoring evaluation is a process of using modern information technology to continually

English translation © 2016 Taylor & Francis, Inc., from the Chinese text "Shuju mijixing pinggu: gaodeng jiaoyu jiance pinggu de neihan, fangfa yu zhanwang" by Wang Zhanjun, Qiao Weifeng, and Li Jiangbo. Translated by Jeff Keller. Originally published in *Jiaoyu yanjiu* [Educational Research], 2015, no. 6 (No. 425 overall), and funded by the National Natural Science Fund General Program "Theoretical and Methodological Research on Higher Education Monitoring Evaluation" (project number: 71273029).

collect and deeply analyze relevant data, visually present the state of higher education, and provide an objective basis for value judgments and scientific decision making by diverse bodies.

Systemic states are the target of monitoring evaluation. States generally refer to "the scope representing the status of a material system. It refers to the method of existence or forms of manifestation of a certain material system during a certain time" (Gao 1988). States are preconditions for people to know things, and without states we cannot know things" (Tao 1998). The state of higher education is the method of existence and forms of manifestation of important elements of the higher education system and their interrelationships within a certain period of time. It is the target of higher education monitoring evaluation, and specifically includes size, speed, quality, structure, and performance.

States can be expressed symbolically using data, and they are measured using scales that mainly have two implications. The first implication is in variables, in which variables are used to measure things, and they mainly include nominal, ordinal, interval, and ratio variables (Stevens 1946). The second implication of scales is in an abstract sense, and indicate from which perspective things are measured. Abstract scales of monitoring evaluation mainly include temporal, spatial, and value scales.

Temporal Scales

Temporal scales are the "pedometers" of status monitoring, and reflect the time distribution and cycles of system statuses in the process of changing, and are often measured using the units of years, seasons, months, weeks, days, and hours. Systems are developing and changing at all times, and all states are the result of the process of accumulation, as today's situation is fostering tomorrow's changes. The choice of temporal scale is related to the stability of the system and directly impacts the overall degree of change in status that is shown. When systemic changes are slower, the monitoring temporal scale can be longer; when systemic changes are quicker, the monitoring temporal scale can be shorter. Modern higher education systems are changing all the time, and evaluations with long cycles cannot clearly reflect the course of changes in systemic states. This requires monitoring evaluation a greater frequency of data collection, greater speed of data updating, and longer uninterrupted period of continuous data collection, which gives higher education monitoring evaluation the characteristic of temporal scale intensity.

Spatial Scales

Spatial scales are the "resolution" of status monitoring and reflect the spatial distribution and extensions of systemic elements and their structures. The choice of spatial scale is related to system complexity and directly impacts the extent to which element characteristics and relationships are revealed. When the system structure and environment are simple, the monitoring spatial scale can be more uniform; when the system structure and environment is complex, the monitoring spatial scale should be diverse. Based on the levels of status elements, the spatial scale can be divided into macro- and microscales, with the former covering the entire situation and the latter covering the details. The status of higher education such as size, speed, quality, structure, and effectiveness is reflected by measuring elements, and some of these elements are on the international, national, or regional macro level, while some are on the institution, subject, specialty, curriculum, teacher or student micro level. Differences in spatial scales are reflected in data granularity. Data granularity is the extent of refinement or comprehensiveness of the data, and greater refinement means smaller granularity, while lower refinement means higher granularity. Data granularity determines the volume of information included, and directly impacts the ability to store, access, and analyze the data. Modern higher education systems are becoming increasingly complex, and they objectively require data with multiple sources, multiple levels, multiple types, and multiple granularities to reflect these features and relationships to help find their hidden rules. Therefore, higher education monitoring evaluation has the features of diverse spatial scales.

Value Scales

Value scales are subjective frames of reference for status, and reflect the anticipated degree of satisfaction of an object toward a subject. The importance of value scales lies in higher education systems being both material and value systems, and performing status monitoring evaluation activities cannot only look at numbers while neglecting people, and cannot overlook "nonmeasurable things." For example, the quality status of higher education must be reflected in facts such as teachers, students, and courses, while the quality level is often determined by the value orientations of the stakeholders (i.e., determined by the concept of quality). Selection of the value scale is more or less related to the number of stakeholders. When there are few stakeholders, the value scale can be less diverse; when there are many stakeholders, the value scale should be more diverse. Modern higher education systems are increasingly more closely connected to the outside world and there are many stakeholders, so value standards should not be "one size fits all." They should respect the value choices of diverse subjects, therefore higher education monitoring evaluation has the feature of diverse value scales.

Systems have different features, and status monitoring has different areas of focus. Monitoring evaluation activities in natural science and engineering technology fields such as bridges, roads, the atmosphere, resources, hydrology, and geology mainly involve material systems, and their status is mainly measured using spatial-temporal scales. Monitoring evaluations for social science fields such as economics, medicine, health, immigration, poverty alleviation, popular opinion, science and technology, and in particular education not only involve material systems, but also involve value systems, so only using spatial-temporal scales is not enough— value scales must also be used for measurement. Therefore, monitoring evaluation in the social science field can draw on the monitoring evaluation methods in the natural science and engineering fields but not completely copy them.

THINKING OF THE PURPOSE: SERVING CONTINUOUS IMPROVEMENT, SCIENTIFIC DECISION MAKING, AND DIVERSE JUDGMENTS

No evaluation activity can avoid the problem of purpose (i.e., the problem of why is the evaluation made and who does it serve) and this problem is sometimes fundamental. "Even though there has been increased communication between those advocating positivistic/quantitative approaches to evaluation and proponents of phenomenological/qualitative approaches, there is a present danger of a polarization developing between these camps. The roots of this polarization are not primarily methodological, but instead reflect ideological differences. (Stufflebeam et al. 2007) Corresponding to the intensity of temporal scales, diversity of spatial scales, and diversity of value scales, the purpose of monitoring evaluation is oriented toward pursing continuous improvement, scientific decision making, and diverse judgments. Serving continuous improvement mainly emphasizes that monitoring evaluations serve educators and learners, serving scientific decision making mainly emphasizes that monitoring evaluations serve policymakers, and serving diverse judgments mainly emphasizes that monitoring evaluations serve society and the public. Figure 1 reflects the features and purpose of monitoring evaluation.

Prompt Feedback of Information, Serving Continuous Improvement

"The purpose of evaluation is to improve, not prove" (Stufflebeam 1983). Systems, organizations, and individuals that want long-term, sustained vigor and vitality must make self-improvements. The essence of improvement is to use positive or negative feedback to adjust and correct the behaviors of organizations and individuals so they conform to the predetermined objectives or establish more reasonable objectives. The possibility and effectiveness of improvements is determined by the timeliness and sustained nature of information feedback. To continually feedback information, one must continually gather and update data. However, traditional external evaluations and accreditation activities in higher education were restricted by conditions such as cost and technology, and often are at intervals of 3–5 years or longer. Some specialized evaluation activities also frequently stop and start, which leads to a serious delay in feedback and difficulties in preserving the "freshness" of information, and this limits their help with continuous improvements. Through information technology measures, monitoring evaluation greatly shrinks the evaluation time scale. The time intervals for data collection

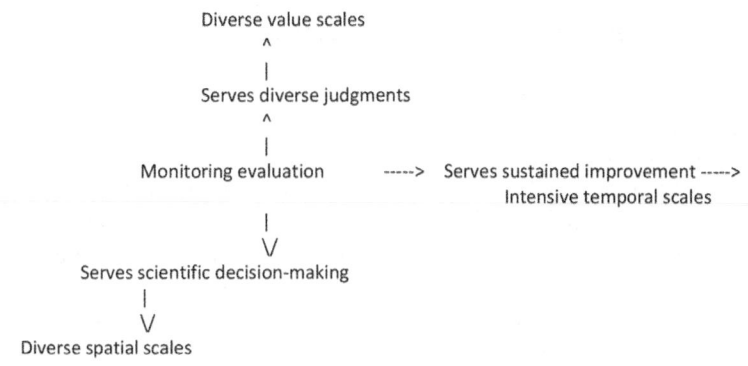

Diagram of scale characteristics and objective orientations of monitoring evaluation

FIGURE 1 Scale characteristics and objective orientations of monitoring evaluation.

and updating shrink to at least one year or less, and some data is collected quarterly, monthly, weekly, daily, or even in real time. This can make complete records and give timely feedback on the state of the evaluation target, discover abnormalities, anticipate trends, and facilitate improvements.

Focusing on Systemic Changes and Serving Scientific Decision Making

The overall feature of modern social development is "going fast," and this requires both continuing and changing. As the pact of higher education massification, internationalization, and marketization picks up speed, higher education systems and institutions are constantly in changing environments, and they need to resolve crises, win competition, seize opportunities, and face challenges and make rapid and scientific policy decisions. However, the internal and external relationships of modern higher education systems are extremely complicated, and intellectual property production, dissemination, and application activities of higher education systems are increasingly inseparable from economic and social development. This demands that higher education decision-makers and managers have systemic thinking and strategic vision. They must focus on changes to the internal status of education systems and also on changes to the external environment of education systems. They must examine the impact of external factors such as social change, market competition, industry development, and policy changes on higher education and improve the level of scientific policy-making. There is a limitation of traditional evaluations, in that it is easy to focus attention on education activities themselves and concentrate on the higher education system without being sensitive to external changes in the environment. It is easy to focus just on the issue at hand, and lack systemic nature. Monitoring evaluation has diversity of spatial scale and values the macro- and microlevels of higher education systems. Data granularity involves every level, and data sources are not limited to within the higher education system and institutions. They are linked with international, regional, and industry data and are helpful in raising the insight and foresight of policy making.

Persisting in Orientation toward Users and Serving Diverse Judgments

Mass higher education facilitated diverse demands for evaluation activities, and higher education monitoring evaluation should provide multidimensional perspectives on observing complex higher education systems and promote the public's right to know, choose, and participate in higher education. Monitoring evaluation both involves factual relations as well as value and behavioral relations. But the key to monitoring evaluation is in resolving the real issue of "what," and draws on technical measures to fully display the characteristics and model of the current state. For the value question of "what should it be," caution and restraint should be maintained and the diverse value choices of stakeholders should be respected, and uniform value scales should not be forced on people. It must be pointed out that monitoring evaluation is a kind of professional activities, and considering the diverse needs of users does not mean being manipulated by the will of users. It prevents hardly discovered misuse of evaluation caused by the combination of quantified evaluation and rights and interests.

CHANGING MODELS: DATA-INTENSIVE EVALUATION

Turing Award winner Jim Gray divided science throughout history into four modes: empirical science, theoretical science, computational science, and eScience or data-intensive science (Gray 2009).[6] Coming along with ubiquitous data collection and computation abilities, data-intensive science is the fourth mode that arises from integrating the first three modes and is differentiated from computational science. The thought of data-intensive science advocates developing data-centered tools that support the entire life cycle (collection, processing, analysis, and visualization) of scientific research data. It advocates putting all scientific literature online, putting all scientific research data online, and having interoperability among them. It also advocates developing a data science with all subjects developing in parallel. This kind of thinking of putting science online and using data to drive scientific discoveries will have a far-reaching impact on the development of all sciences. In recent years, data-intensive science has shown a bright future in the fields of natural science and engineering research. Both *Nature* and *Science* had special issues discussing the development of "big data" and its impact on scientific research (Nature 1997). Microsoft Research had scientists publish a book discussing advancements of the fourth model in the fields of earth and environmental science, life and health science, and data information infrastructure (Hey et al. 2015). Furthermore, new branches in the field of social science have arisen that are characterized by their data-intensive nature, such as computational sociology (Lazer et al. 2009), data-driven journalism (Gray et al. 2012), and learning analytics, which has arisen recently along with massive open online courses (MOOC; Buckingham 2015). Some scholars established the International Educational Data Mining Society in 2011, which focuses on data mining in education environments to better understand the behavior of learners (International Educational Data Mining Society).

The thought of data-intensive science is enlightening for carrying out higher education monitoring evaluation, and in this article the definition of monitoring evaluation is synonymous with data-driven evaluation or data-intensive evaluation.

Higher Education Monitoring Evaluation is Data-Driven Evaluation

Data-driven evaluation refers to using evaluation data to reveal the relationships of element features and structures in the status of higher education, and is not mainly based on expert judgments. Monitoring evaluation emphasizes letting the data speak, and the evaluation conclusion is revealed by in-depth data analysis. It uses modern information technology to ensure the professional nature of the evaluation, and relies on technical rules of data processing to ensure the standardized nature of the evaluation. Traditional evaluations are mainly expert-driven and the evaluation process relies on experts. The evaluation conclusions mainly rely on the judgments of experts based on their "convictions," and use the reasoning, knowledge, and experience of the experts to ensure the professional nature of the evaluations and use procedural rules such as voting, challenges, and disclosure to guarantee the standardized nature of the evaluations. Being data-driven not only uses data as evidence for evaluation conclusions, but more importantly it finds the patterns of higher education activities reflected in the data to guide education policy-making, institution management, and the behavior of educators and students.

Monitoring evaluation does not deny the role of experts, because after all computers cannot completely replace human thinking and data can also lie, and expert experience must play a guiding role in evaluation design, data collection, analysis, and interpretation. But monitoring evaluation does not rely on experts making terminal conclusions and does not completely hand the judgment rights over to experts. Instead, it upholds the leading position of technical analysis and lets data play the leading role to effectively decrease the subjective arbitrariness of expert-driven evaluations and prevent ethical risks and more reasonably make use of the professional wisdom of experts. Data-driven evaluation and expert-driven evaluation each have their advantages and limitations and should be mutually instructive and complimentary.

Higher Education Monitoring Evaluation is Data-intensive Evaluation

The foundation for higher education monitoring evaluation is "big data" but not "small data". Some researchers and institutions use "3 V" (volume, velocity, and variety; META Group 2015). and "4 V" (3 V + value or veracity; Hamish 2015) to describe the features of "big data." These features are different summaries of the temporal, spatial, and value features of "big data," and the features of monitoring evaluation scales are interlinked with the above features of "big data."

There are major differences between monitoring evaluation and quantity evaluation based on "small data." Quantity evaluations in the "small data" era used data to help experts make judgments or verify theoretical hypotheses in pursuit of obtaining greater volumes of information from fewer data. They often followed scientific sampling, demanded that data be structured, and valued drawing inferences from the causal relationships among variables. Monitoring evaluations based on "big data" or "quasi big data" explore the features, relationships, and models concealed in the data. This kind of exploration is a process of repeated iterations and often surpasses what can be directly perceived or experienced.

Of course, "big data" and "small data" are relative concepts, and the size of data is related to the sample space and the proportion of unstructured data and streaming data, and different fields also have different standards. The core differences between "big data" and "small data" evaluations is in the size of the data and in the methods and thinking they each follow. Monitoring evaluation advocates "big data" thinking in pursuit of using all samples but not random samples, accepting the heterogeneity of the data but not pursuing accuracy, and focusing more on correlations but not causal relationships (Mayer-Schönberger and Cukier 2013).

How is data-intensive evaluation possible in higher education? Along with the rapid development of information technology and internet and rapid move to IT-based higher education, there has been an exponential growth in the data in higher education field, and the era of "big data" in higher education is upon us. Apart from monitoring databases for the status of higher education, this data also includes continuously generating openly available data such as data on institution management, teaching, research, learning behavior in MOOC, large-scale standard test, large-scale questionnaire surveys, social networks, news reporting, economics, science and technology, and population. As the degree of data sharing increases and modern information technology is developed and applied in the higher education field, more and more the value of these data could be explored.

On the whole, the redefined evaluation here is different from traditional expert-driven evaluation and different from quantity evaluation based on "small data," and instead it is a data-based exploration, that is a "journey of discovery."

THE JOURNEY OF DISCOVERY: BASED ON MODERN INFORMATION TECHNOLOGY

Using monitoring evaluation as a meaningful journey of discovery requires getting help from modern information technology. Modern information technology is a general term for various hardware and software technology that uses computers to manage and process information. Modern information technology is attempting to model human knowledge and thinking, exploring the internal pattern of things within large volumes of data, and helping people to analyze and judge complex problems. The three conditions of materials, tools, and people must be met for monitoring evaluation, namely a large volume of data, data mining and visualization technology, and education experts and data analysts. Technologies toolkit in higher education monitoring evaluation can be mainly summed up as the three areas of data collection and consolidation, data mining and analysis, and data visualization.

Data Collection and Consolidation

Data collection and consolidation technology mainly resolves raw material problems for monitoring evaluation, and emphasizes building databases and data warehouses. The data that monitoring evaluation relies on is different from general statistical data, and it must have enough size, depth, and consolidation. In terms of size, using high frequency or even online real-time data collection methods helps the overall size of the data rapidly accumulate and grow. In terms of depth, gradually realizing data multigranularity allows for not only the inclusion of macro-level data on the international, national, and regional level, but also can include microlevel data on the institution, subject, specialty, curriculum, and individual level, which provides data sources for in-depth mining of possible data connections. Consolidation requires converging dispersed data in different business systems into one ocean, forming a data warehouse suitable for data mining on a subject.

Currently, the Higher Education Evaluation Center of Ministry of Education has built a database on the basic state of undergraduate education. The data is organized based on institution and year, and includes the seven major categories of basic institution information, basic institution conditions, subject and specialties, teacher information, talent cultivation, student information, and teaching management and quality control, with a total of 572 indicators (Education Evaluation Center of the Ministry of Education). This database realizes fine information granularity on the spatial scale with information on individual teachers and information on individual. On the temporal scale it improves timeliness and includes a large volume of online immediately reported timing data. This provides support for smoothly undertaking the latest round of institutions review for newly built undergraduate colleges and review for general undergraduate universities, and lays a foundation for performing higher education monitoring evaluation.

One major difficulty in monitoring evaluation is the problem of data sources. Forming "big data" requires the Internet, which means building monitoring evaluation platforms based on cloud computing. The platforms are based on database technology and Internet technology, and gradually integrate functions such as data collection, storage, analysis, and visualization into the cloud, so that institutions do not have to build dedicated servers and can use desktop terminals to access the status database online. They also must develop cloud-based software applications to support mobile terminal data collection, queries, and personalized recommendations.

The key problem in platform construction of evaluation cloud is not mainly in technology and cost, but rather in concepts and cooperation. To encourage thousands of higher education institutions to participate in platform building, we first must let institutions who share data benefit from it. The building of evaluation cloud platforms should advocate the concept of joint construction and sharing, and give equal sharing rights to data contributors based on laws and agreements. At the same time, assignments can be accepted for providing more personalized, precise, and professional data analysis services. Furthermore, based on their own needs, higher education institutions can also consolidate internal and external data on education, research, and management scattered in various departments, build a routine monitoring data warehouse for subject and specialties, and carry out internal monitoring evaluation activities. These have important value for teaching reforms, specialty adjustments, and management innovation.

Data Mining and Analysis

Data excavation and analysis technology mainly resolves problems of value abstraction in the data set, and data mining is the main method. Data mining is also called data archaeology, data prospecting, and data dredging. It is the "evolution of information technology" (Han and Kamber 2012), and a "non-trivial process of discovering valid, significant, potentially useful, and easily perceived data models from a large volume of data automatically or semi-automatically" (Fayyad et al. 1996). In a broad sense, data mining and knowledge discovery in databases are basically synonymous. In a narrow sense, data mining is a basic step in knowledge discovery, and apart from this, it also includes data cleaning, data integration, data selection, data transformation, model evaluation, and knowledge representation.

In monitoring evaluation, the greatest challenge in applying data mining is how to find and develop models, algorithms, and tools suitable for monitoring the state of higher education. Based on the features of the targets, subjects of evaluation, and data types and sizes, monitoring evaluation should comprehensively apply measures such as on-line analysis processing, data mining, machine learning, and artificial neural networks, find value in large amounts of data, explore real states, anticipate future trends, and increase people's rational knowledge of the state and inner rules of higher education.

Data Visualization

If we say that data mining resolves the problem of "in-depth analysis" monitoring evaluation, data visualization resolves problems of simply "presentation." Data visualization is a new discipline developed on the foundation of computer graphics, visual design, and human-computer interaction (HCI) techniques, emphasizes transmitting abstract information in a visual method, advances people's understanding of data, and plays a unique role in increasing knowledge, reducing searching, improving memory, and making inferences.

In an information society, conflicts of information asymmetry and information overload continually exist. On the one hand, people want to understand richer information. On the other hand, as soon as information surpasses the scope of processing, understanding, or use of individuals and systems, it causes a disturbance in the process of human understanding. In the field of evaluation, the huge volume of statistical information and continuous streams of evaluation reports often create a buildup of information that increases people's difficulties in understanding. Monitoring evaluation values the application of information visualization technology, draws on various visualization tools, and directly and clearly reflects the state of higher education. Similar to an outstanding artist, the issue is not in how it piles up materials for viewers, but rather in eliminating the unimportant parts of the materials and presenting people with clear, vivid images that reflect reality.

Hardcopy and electronic reports in monitoring evaluation should widely use data visualization technology to stimulate readers' senses and clearly and effectively transmit and communicate information. They also should respect the technical standards of information visualization, correctly display the original appearance of the data, and avoid misleading people. Data visualization technology already plays a large role in university rankings. For example, the European Union–funded U-Multirank project (Van Vught and Ziegele 2012) uses online, visual, interactive, refined data presentation methods, provides users with richer and more valuable information, and to a certain extent limits the bad practice of using comprehensive indicators.

It must be pointed out that in monitoring evaluation, we cannot put the cart before the horse and choose the evaluation purpose and problems based on the methodology, but rather choose an appropriate methodology based on the evaluation objective and problems. Being data-intensive is a significant feature of monitoring evaluation, and its method system should be open and not closed. As modern information technology develops, new methods and tools will continually be incorporated into the monitoring evaluation method system.

REFLECTIONS AND PROSPECTS

Technology, concepts, and systems are three key drivers affecting higher education evaluation. The "Education Plan Outline" clearly calls for integrating national education quality monitoring evaluation institutions and resources and improving the monitoring evaluation system. "Opinions of Ministry of Education on Undergraduate Education Evaluation Work for General Higher Education Institutions" issued in 2011 makes routine monitoring of status data an important, integral part of the higher education evaluation system. Building a monitoring evaluation system and increasing policy choices for monitoring evaluation capabilities can reflect urgently needed changes in higher education evaluation in China and suits the need for systemic changes and governance reforms in higher education.

Need to Adapt to Changes in the Higher Education System

The role of higher education in increasing individual opportunities, forming an organization mission, promoting social development, and realizing national strategy is readily apparent.

Since the turn of the century, as the result of the joint efforts of internal and external forces, the higher education systems in China and many countries around the world underwent enormous changes. Massification gradually advanced and deepened, the impact of market factors continually expanded, international cooperation and exchange has just begun, and information and network technology is more broadly applied. These reforms are changing the state and appearance of higher education, the higher education system is becoming larger and more complex, and assuring the quality of higher education and improving competitiveness in higher education has become the common focus of government authorities, education institutions, the public, and markets. The increasing complexity of higher education systems and diverse demands of stakeholders requires remaining highly sensitive to the evolving state of higher education systems and effectively helping different stakeholders perceive such changes from multiple perspectives. This is the background under which higher education monitoring evaluation was produced.

Need to Adapt to Changes in Higher Education Governance

The governance structure of higher education in China is undergoing major adjustments. On the one hand, higher education systems are gradually moving from highly centralized government authority to provincial-level planning, university autonomy, and grassroots autonomy. On the other hand, the power of higher education academic organizations, industry associations, and professionally organized academics is continually growing, and there is initial development in social third-party evaluation organizations. Modern public administrative reforms in the Chinese government are the political foundation generating such changes. These reforms are built on the foundation of Chinese practice and also are affected by modern Western concepts of governance. They emphasize that the government must reasonably position and transform duties, lie somewhere between doing everything and not doing anything, and in the end establish a limited and effective service government. Looking at the experiences of developed countries, building a modern university system is an important channel for improving the governance ability of higher education.

In China, the first task in establishing a modern university system is using decentralization of power to realize relative separation of management, operation and evaluation, and gradually forming a state of higher education governance with diverse participation by government, universities, and the market (society). After the gradual removal of direct government interference, the importance of effective evaluation becomes increasingly evident, and higher education monitoring evaluation provides policy-makers with new tools for promptly and accurately understanding their own advantages and disadvantages and discovering potential crises and opportunities.

Currently, the theoretical research and practical activities of higher education monitoring evaluation are in the initial exploration stage and face challenges.

Challenges Facing Evaluation Data

Data is becoming a strategic resource and core competitive force. Even though the country has established a database on the basic status of undergraduate education and has initially applied it in practice, it is still a certain distance from "big data" and needs the strong support and active participation of all levels of government authorities, higher education institutions, and third party organizations. Apart from actively promoting the prompt publication of public information of government authorities and higher education institutions, the state needs to start from an overall informatization strategy, focus on building and integrating higher education information databases, and seize on opportunities in forming and applying education big data. At the same time, it should focus on issues of information privacy and security. Currently, some Western university ranking organizations have already started inviting Chinese higher education institutions to provide education data, and this is a phenomenon that needs to be given attention.

Challenges for Professional Personnel

Performing monitoring evaluation not only requires a large number of highly experienced education workers, it also requires a large number of data analysts who understand education. This is a precondition and key part of turning monitoring evaluation into a professional activity. Performing monitoring evaluation will attract participation of some third-party organizations good at data analysis, and higher education institutions with the greatest advantage in talent cultivation will also cultivate many professional personnel to carry out monitoring evaluation activities. This has especially important significance for improving education and improving the professional and scientific level of education management and policy making. It can be anticipated that the integration of technical and education experts will contribute more to grasping the patterns of higher education and advancing its development.

Challenges for Evaluation Concepts

Accepting new things requires a process. Traditional professionally driven evaluation has already left a stiff impression in the field of higher education, and there is a large conceptual difference between this kind of new evaluation category of monitoring education and traditional evaluation. A long process is necessary to identify it in concept and practice. But if sharp managers fully recognize and understand the new concepts and methods in this new category of evaluation, rapidly transform their concepts, and promote the application of monitoring evaluation in higher education, this will have a positive impact on the reform and development of higher education.

Education evaluation is one of the most direct and important fields of application of education big data. The historical intersection of the development of modern information technology and massification of higher education has provided new opportunities and challenges for performing data-intensive higher education monitoring evaluation. There are many problems that still await resolution in this field that require theoretical and methodological support and policy assurance and concept consensus. The active participation by academic communities and stakeholders will undoubtedly promote the continued in-depth development of this field.

REFERENCES

Buckingham, S. S. 2015. *UNESCO Learning Analytics Policy Brief.* http//iite.unesco.org/pics/publications/en/files/3214711.pdf. (Accessed March 30, 2015).

Education Evaluation Center of the Ministry of Education. 2014. Guojia gaoxiao benke jiaoxue jiben zhuangtai shujuku shuju biaoge ji neihan shuoming (Data tables and an explanation of their contents from the national database on the Basic State of College Undergraduate Education) (version 2.0.5). http://udb.heec.edu.cn/smartbi/vision/neihan.pdf (Accessed March 30, 2015).

Fayyad, U., G. Piatetsky-Shapiro, and P. Smyth. 1996. From data mining to knowledge discovery in databases. *AI Magazine* (3).

Gao, Q. 1988. *Wenshizhe baike cidian [Encyclopedic dictionary of literature, philosophy, and history]*, 385. Jilin: Jilin daxue chubanshe.

Gray, J. 2009. *A Transformed Scientific Method.* http//research.microsoft.com/enus/collaboration/fourthparadigm/4th_paradigm_book_jim_gray_transcript.pdf. (Accessed March 30, 2015).

Gray, J., L. Chambers, and L. Bounegru. 2012. *The Data Journalism Handbook.* Sebastopol, CA: O'Reilly Media.

Hamish, B. 2015. *The 'four Vs' of Big Data.* http://www.computerworld.com.au/article/396198/iiis_four_vs_big_data/. (Accessed March 30, 2015).

Han, J., and M. Kamber. 2012. *Shuju wajue gainian yu jishu (Data mining concepts and techniques)*, ed. Y. Yang, 2–4. Beijing: Jixie gongye chubanshe.

Hey, T., S. Tansley, and K. Tolle. (Eds.). 2015. *The Fourth Paradigm: Data-Intensive Scientific Discovery.* Redmond, WA: Microsoft Research.

International Educational Data Mining Society. 2015. About. http://www.educationaldatamining.org/about. (Accessed May 11, 2015).

Lazer, D., A. Pentland, L. Adamic, S. Aral, A.-L. Barabási, D. Brewer, N. Christakis, N. Contractor, J. Fowler, M. Gutmann, T. Jebara, G. King, M. Macy, D. Roy, and M. Van Alstyne. 2009. Social science: Computational social science. *Science* 323, 721–723.

Madaus, G. F., M. Scriven, and D. L. Stufflebeam. (Eds.) 2007. *Pinggu moxing [Evaluation models]*, 19. Beijing: Beijing daxue chubanshe.

Mayer-Schönberger, V., and K. Cukier. 2013. *Dashuju shidai: Shenghuo, gongzuo yu siwei de dabiange [Big data: A revolution that will transform how we live, work, and think]*, 29. Hangzhou: Zhejiang renmin chubanshe.

META Group. 2015. *3D Data Management: Controlling Data Volume, Velocity, and Variety.* http://blogs.gartner.com/douglaney/files/2012/01/ad949-3D-Data-Management-Controlling-Data-Volume-Velocity-and-Variety.pdf. (Accessed March 30, 2015).

Stevens, S. S. 1946. On the theory of scales of measurement. *Science* 103, 677–680.

Stufflebeam, D. L. 1983. The CIPP Model for Program Evaluation. In Madaus G. F., Scriven, M. S., Stufflebeam, D. L. (Eds.), Evaluation Models. Boston, MA: Kluwer.

Tao, X. 1998. *Jiaoyu pingjia cidian [Dictionary of education evaluation]*, 51–52. Beijing: Beijing shifan daxue chubanshe.

Van Vught, F. A., and F. Ziegele. (Eds.). 2012. *Multidimensional Ranking: The Design and Development of U-Multirank.* Dordrecht, the Netherlands: Springer.

The Evolution of Topics and Leading Trends over the Past 15 Years of Research on the Quality of Higher Education in China: Based on Keyword Co-Occurrence Knowledge Map Analysis of the Research Papers Published from 2000 to 2014 in the CSSCI Database

Qu Xia and Yang Xiaotong

Abstract: Using CiteSpace to draw a keyword co-occurrence knowledge map for 1,048 research papers on the quality of higher education from 2000 to 2014 in the Chinese Social Sciences Citation Index database, we found that over the past 15 years, research on the quality of Chinese higher education was clearly oriented toward policies, and a good interactive relationship formed between research and policy. Looking at research topics, apart from macrodiscussions of the spirit of several educational reforms, the relevant topics are mainly focused on higher education quality issues in the massification stage, issues of higher education academic management, issues of student cultivation, and issues of ensuring and evaluating higher education quality. Of these, issues of ensuring and evaluating higher education quality have continually been the mainstream of research on Chinese higher education quality, and there has been an increasing trend of emphasizing ensuring internal quality within schools, emphasizing student participation, and evaluating the effectiveness of student learning. Scholars had a renewed focus on the topics of higher education academic management and student cultivation after 2010, and truly improving the quality of higher education will become a future hot topic of study, however there is an urgent need for further study.

Since the 1999 expansion in higher education recruitment, the quality of higher education has continually been a topic of much focus in China's academic world. Some scholars calculate that relevant research papers have surged for many years since 2000 at rates greater than exponential growth (Qiu and Ai 2013). The 2010 "State Mid- to Long-Term Educational Reform and

English translation © 2016 Taylor & Francis, Inc., from the Chinese text "Zhongguo gaodeng jiaoyu zhiliang yanjiu shiwunian de huati yanjin yu qianyan qushi—jiyu CSSCI shujuku 2000–2014 nian lunwen guanjianci gongxian zhishi tupu fenxi" by Qu Xia and Yang Xiaotong. Translated by Jeff Keller. Originally published in *Zhongguo gaojiao yanjiu* [China Higher Education Research], 2015, no. 9, and funded by the Beijing City Social Sciences Fund Key Project "Theoretical and Empirical Research on High-Quality Undergraduate Education Supported by Scientific Research" (project no. 14JYA002).
Color versions of one or more figures in the article can be found online at www.tandfonline.com/mced.

Development Plan Outline 2010–2020" (Guojia zhongchangqi jiaoyu gaige he fazhan guihua gangyao 2010–2020) (hereinafter "Educational Plan Outline") even more clearly pointed out that "improving quality is the core task of developing higher education and a basic requirement for building a country with strong higher education." From this we can infer that for a long time to come, the problem of quality of higher education will still be a hot topic in the world of higher education. Then, what basic topics have studies on higher education quality over the past 15 years mainly focused on? What are their interrelationships? Which topics are at the forefront of current research on the quality of Chinese higher education? What will future research look at? By answering these questions, we not only can deeply understand the progress and drawbacks already obtained in academic research on higher education quality, they can also provide us lessons and references for further studies.

RESEARCH METHODS AND DESIGN

Research Methods

Past discussions of research on higher education quality mainly followed two paths: one was using traditional textual analytical methods to make overall analyses and evaluations of existing research articles on higher education quality. An early and influential study in this regard was Qiu Meisheng's 2002 article "An Overview of Research on the Quality of Mass Higher Education" (Qiu 2002). Similar research was also performed by Qu and Meng (2008), Yan (2011), and Wu and Chen (2012), and by deeply reading and analyzing certain articles, they summarized the basic views in the main fields of research on Chinese higher education. The second was using quantitative textual analysis methods to perform objective statistical analysis on the overall state of research papers on higher education quality during a certain period with regard to aspects such as publication dates, authors, organizations, cited works, and keywords, and gave an overall picture of research on the quality of Chinese higher education. This is a new research path that has appeared in the past few years, and representative works include the articles published by Qiu and Ai (2013), Qiu and Lou (2013), and Liu and Wu (2014) in 2013 and 2014. Even though the second method can do a good job making up for the drawbacks of traditional textual analysis that tended to be qualitative and highly subjective, most of such studies stopped at descriptive statistics of various external objective information about the articles, and it is difficult for them to deeply reveal the substantial topics of existing research and their mutual relationships.

Knowledge mapping is a diagram that shows the developmental progress and structural relationships for a field of scientific knowledge, "with the dual attributes and characteristics of an 'image' and 'map': both a visualizable knowledge diagram and an orderable knowledge genealogy, it shows many hidden complex relationships such as networks, structures, interactions, intersections, evolutions, and derivations of knowledge units or knowledge groups, and such complex relationships foster the generation of new knowledge" (Chen and Chen et al. 2014). CiteSpace is visualization software developed by Professor Chen Chaomei from Drexel University. It is currently one of the most widely applied scientific knowledge mapping tools, and can transform a large textual database into a visualized knowledge map, thereby visualizing the patterns and hardly perceived phenomena that are hidden within a large amount of data. This study used the latest version of CiteSpace v.3.9 R8 (64-bit) to create a scientific knowledge map of research on the quality of Chinese higher education over the past 15 years and also uses a secondary literature method to review key articles and discover the basic topics explored by Chinese academics in this field, their structural networks, and their derivative and evolutionary relationships.

Research Samples

This study uses the Chinese Social Sciences Citation Index (CSSCI) which includes articles that are highly influential and have strong academics and norms as a sample source database. Even though the CSSCI has far fewer articles than CNKI, Bradford's law shows that the key articles in one field are concentrated in a small number of core periodicals. Therefore, the CSSCI database centrally collects key results of research on Chinese higher education quality. We used "higher education quality" as the "subject" search, "OR" as the search relationship, and "keywords" that included both "higher education" and "quality" as search conditions, and found 1,074 articles published from 2000 to 2014 in the CSSCI, and the publication volume for each year can be seen in Figure 1. After removing articles such as conference reviews and notices, we kept 1,048 articles reflecting the substantial content of research on Chinese higher education quality, and preprocessed the data using the format converter that came with CiteSpace.

Research Indicators

This study mainly captures the topics and leading trends of research on Chinese higher education quality over the past 15 years from the cited texts. Specifically, it uses a co-word analysis and cluster analysis of terms and keywords in the cited texts combined with a second reading of

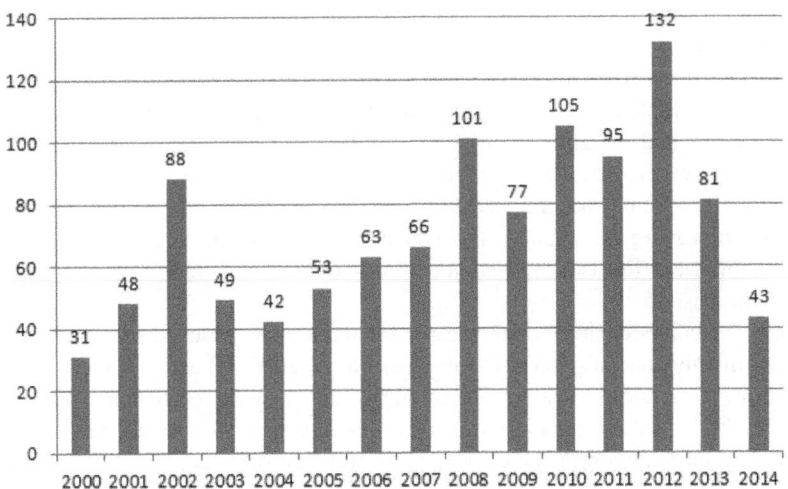

FIGURE 1 Publication volume of research papers on higher education quality by year from 2000 to 2014.

the texts to confirm the main topics, structural relationships, and diachronic development of research on Chinese higher education quality; by finding and tracking burst terms, it determines the leading subjects at different times.

KNOWLEDGE MAP OF THE CO-OCCURRENCE OF KEYWORDS IN RESEARCH ARTICLES ON HIGHER EDUCATION QUALITY

This study first performed a co-word analysis of keywords and subject words from articles that met the study requirements among the 1,048 obtained from the CSSCI. As an important analytical technique for textual content, co-word analysis "analyses commonly occurring forms of item pairs (word or noun phrase pairs) in the same textual subject to confirm the relationships among relevant subjects in the field represented by the article, and further exploring the development of the field" (Pan and Wang 2011). After starting CiteSpace, we selected the time span of 2000–2014 in "Time Slicing"; selected 3-year time intervals with a total of five time intervals in "Years Per Slice"; selected node type as "term" and "keyword" in "Node Type"; and for threshold value selected "Top N Per Slice" as system default value 50, that is, selected the first fifty keywords by frequency to appear within each time interval for targets of analysis, and constructed a knowledge map of keyword co-occurrence.

After forming an initial map through the visualization operation, we discovered that "higher education" was at the top of the word list with a frequency of 620, and covered all nodes of the map, and next came "education quality" and "higher education quality" with frequencies of 313 and 229, respectively. We believe that this is closely related to the search-style setup of this study. These three high-frequency words ensured the accuracy of this study's search scope, but cannot reflect the specific contents of the articles. Therefore, in the final map display, I eliminated these three keyword nodes, and also combined some nodes that clearly expressed the same meanings, such as "higher education massification," "massification," and "mass higher education"; "America," "American education," and "American higher education"; and "British higher education" and "Britain," forming a keyword co-occurrence map with 164 nodes and 177 connections (see Figure 2).

Figure 2 shows node markers for frequencies over five and centrality greater than 0.1 in the field of research on higher education quality over the past 15 years. The greater the frequency the larger the node, and the greater the centrality the more clear the purple circle.

From the figure we can see that the three most prominent nodes are education quality, quality assurance, and higher education massification. We can see that in the stage of higher education massification, improving the quality of higher education teaching and assuring the quality of higher education were the two mainstream topics of research on Chinese higher education quality over the past 15 years.

Looking at the colors of the annual rings of the three main nodes, discussions of "education quality" were mainly concentrated in the two periods of 2000–02 and 2003–05, and apparently there were more discussions of this problem during the early period of mass higher education. The keyword "higher education massification" was mainly concentrated before 2009, and its usage frequency subsequently had a clear decline. We can see that after ten years of expanded recruitment, people saw higher education massification as a natural context that need not be mentioned in discussions of problems of higher education quality. Discussions of "quality

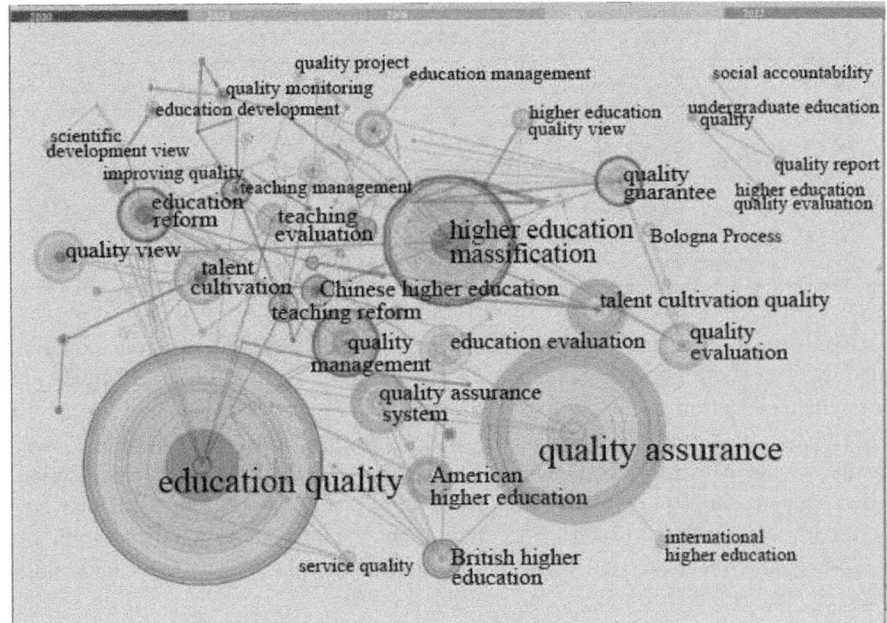

FIGURE 2 Knowledge map of the co-occurrence of keywords in research articles on higher education quality from 2000 to 2014.

assurance" started around 2003, and reached a peak during the 2009–11 period. It was discussed frequently after 2012 as well, and it can be regarded as a mainstream of the past 15 years of research on higher education quality.

Apart from these three main nodes, quality guarantee, quality management, quality assurance system, quality evaluation, education evaluation, American higher education, and British higher education were also large nodes with many interconnections which shows a close co-word relationship among them, and they jointly formed a mainstream of higher education quality management and assurance. Looking at the colors of these keyword nodes and connections, the keyword "quality guarantee" mainly appeared before 2009, while after 2009 keywords such as "quality assurance," "quality assurance system," and "quality evaluation" were used more. Apparently, as some scholars have analyzed, even though "quality guarantee" and "quality assurance" are used in the same way, and come from the English phrase "quality assurance," considering that higher education quality is more of a kind of "soft power," it is more apt to use the word "assurance" when the government is the main entity in charge of higher education quality (Li et al. 2008). Therefore, "quality assurance" became the more common usage in 2009.

The nodes "teaching management," "teaching reform," and "teaching evaluation" have close co-word relationships to "education quality." Looking at the colors of these nodes, such research was mainly concentrated before 2009. Apart from this, "talent cultivation quality," "talent cultivation," "education reform," and "quality view" were large nodes, which shows that they were also important topics in research of Chinese higher education quality.

TABLE 1
Keywords of Centrality 0.2 and above and their Frequencies

No.	Keywords	Centrality	Appearance frequencies
1	Education reform	0.25	47
2	Education administration	0.24	24
3	Quality guarantee	0.22	45
4	Quality management	0.21	58
5	Higher education massification	0.21	108
6	Education quality	0.2	198

It is worth mentioning that in the upper right corner of the map are four nodes that are separated from the main knowledge map and form their own system. They are "quality report," "undergraduate education quality," "higher education quality evaluation," and "social accountability." Looking at the colors of the nodes and connecting lines, they appeared after 2012. Apparently as the Ministry of Education's new project of undergraduate education work evaluation appeared in 2011, research on the role and effectiveness of undergraduate education quality report appeared. But such research did not establish a relationship with previous research on higher education quality assurance or education quality, and it appeared rather late, has relatively few research findings, and has small nodes.

Figure 2 also uses purple circles to mark keyword nodes with high centrality. The clearer the purple represents a greater centrality for the keyword and the more nodes with co-word relationships. Nodes with high frequency and centrality often have more key positions in the entire knowledge map and more easily become nodes for consolidating or linking different clusters. Table 1 lists keyword nodes with high frequencies and centrality.

MAIN TOPICS AND THEIR EVOLUTION IN 15 YEARS OF RESEARCH ON CHINESE HIGHER EDUCATION QUALITY

The CiteSpace clustering function uses the proximity of nodes to divide nodes with clear co-word relationships into different categories. Each category can be regarded as a basic topic made up of subject words or keywords that commonly occur within one group. During clustering, on the basis of removing and consolidating the above keywords, the authors first chose the system default Top 50 for clustering. However, it was difficult to see natural clusters in the map that was formed, and the nodes in the clusters formed using the CiteSpace calculation were tied up with one another, and it was difficult to untangle them. After repeated adjustment, the authors discovered that when setting the threshold value (c cc ccv) at 4, 4, and 20, which means that clustering was made for keywords that appeared more than four times, co-occurred more than four times, and had similarity coefficients greater than 0.20 in each time period, and the generated map had a clearer structure, and the module values and average contour values were more reasonable. Therefore, using this threshold value setup, after further consolidating keywords that express similar meanings in this study such as "quality guarantee" and "quality assurance" and "quality view" and "higher education quality view," and using the "Pathfinder" pruning, we performed clustering using the "find optimal clusters" method and used "keywords" as the cluster labels. We used the TF*IDF weighted calculation, and chose the keywords with the greatest weighted values to indicate the subject of each cluster. This formed a knowledge map with 95 nodes, 81 connecting lines, and six main clusters (see Figure 3). Figure 4 provides a timeline for all cluster formation. Through the timeline we can more clearly reflect the years in which the clusters started to appear (when related keywords met our set threshold value), the years in which research findings increased (the nodes have the thickest-colored year ring during this period), and the years in which research interest started to decline.

The clustering results indicate that research on Chinese higher education quality over the past 15 years mainly focused on six main subjects: higher education institutions assuring "education quality," discussions of higher education quality under the background of "education reforms," higher education "quality evaluation," higher education "teaching management," "talent cultivation," and "quality view" of higher education under the background of massification.

Assuring "education quality" in higher education was the largest category and included sixteen nodes. Not only did scholars focus on problems of education quality in General higher education institutions, but also many articles discussed quality and effectiveness problems in "adult higher education," "international higher education," and "Chinese-foreign cooperative education." The second literature review found that issues of government's power and responsibilities in education quality assurance and supervision of all types of higher education

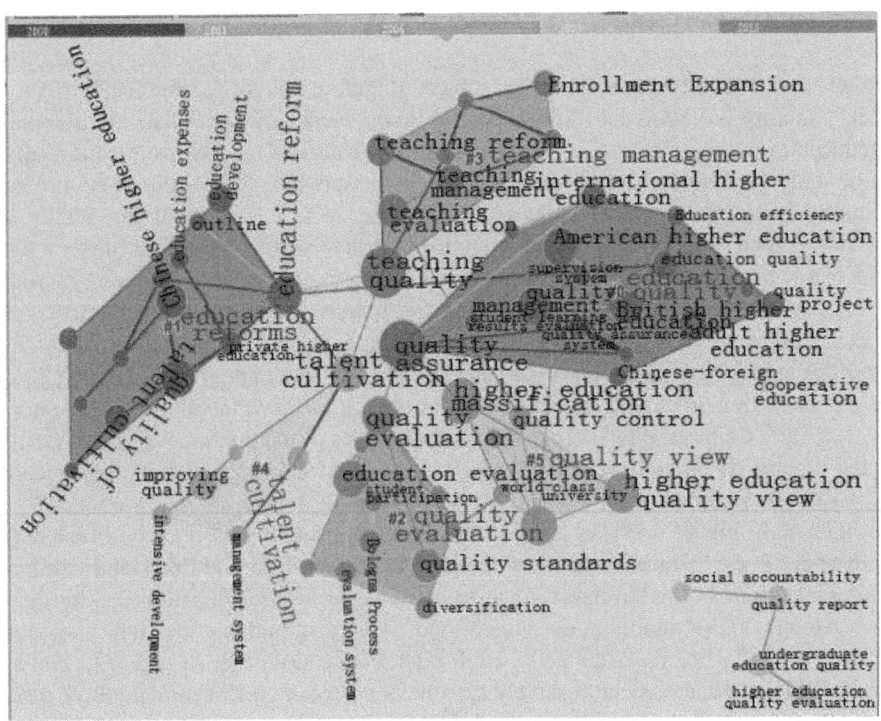

FIGURE 3 Keyword cluster knowledge map of research on higher education quality from 2000 to 2014.

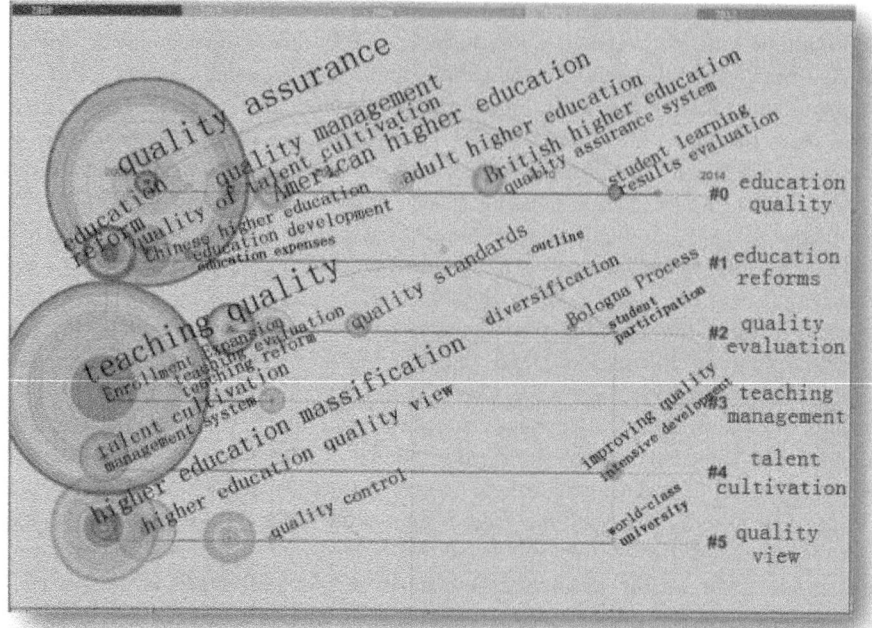

FIGURE 4 Keyword cluster timeline of research on higher education quality from 2000 to 2014.

institutions were discussed the most in this subject, therefore "quality assurance," "quality management," "quality project," and "supervision system" were keywords that often appeared at
high frequencies in this subject. The United States and United Kingdom were continually main
targets of study for Chinese higher education quality assurance. The second literature analysis
found that early on scholars mainly focused on the macropolicy level including quality accreditation, quality management, and quality assurance mechanisms of American higher education.
Chinese scholars also paid attention to the "student learning results evaluation" of American
universities focusing on production and using the quality management method of "directly
facing the added value of student learning and stressing evidence of educational outcomes" that
became a "changing trend in quality assurance models of world universities" (Huang 2013). On
the basis of reflecting on inadequacies of previous undergraduate education assessment work in
China, after 2009 Chinese scholars focused on the features of the prevalence of university autonomy and organic integration of internal and external controls in the British higher education
quality assurance system.

The timeline in Figure 4 shows that in this clustering, "quality assurance (guarantee)" was
the main node in the "education quality" cluster. It appeared around 2001 and continued up
to the present, and was the strongest voice in research on higher education quality these past
15 years. Around 2003, "quality management" and "American higher education" started attract-
ing the attention of scholars. After 2006, adult higher education, British higher education, and
international higher education successively became hot topics in "education quality" assurance,
and "evaluation of student learning results" was the far right node that appeared last in this
cluster.

"Education reform" was the second major cluster, and included thirteen nodes. From the line colors in Figure 3 and Figure 4 we can see that many keywords in this cluster appeared during the 2000–02 period, such as "Chinese higher education," "quality of talent cultivation," "private higher education," "private universities," "education development," and "education expenses." This is because expanded higher education recruitment in China occurred under the promotion of the two educational reform documents "Education Revitalization Action Plan for the 21st Century" and "Decision to Deepen Educational Reforms to Comprehensively Advance Quality Education" in 1999. The proposal of these documents to raise the higher education enrollment rate to 15% by 2010 and continually improve the quality of education while improving the economy of higher education scale led to raising educational expenses through multiple channels and strongly developing private education, and realizing the win-win situation of the scale of "education development" and "quality of talent development." This became a hotly discussed topic among scholars from 2000 to 2005, and relevant discussions diminished thereafter. The last keyword to appear in this cluster was "outline," which means that the 2010 issuance of the "Education Plan Outline" constituted the reform background for further discussions of problems of higher education quality. We can see that "education reform" was the macropolicy background for the past 15 years of discussions of Chinese higher education quality, therefore it became the keyword with the greatest intermediary connections, and also a node connecting the three main clusters of "education quality," "education quality," and "talent cultivation."

"Quality evaluation" was the third main cluster, and included eleven nodes and connects to "education quality" through the "quality assurance" node. The main keywords of this cluster were "quality evaluation" and "education evaluation." Looking at the Figure 4 timeline, these two keywords both met the threshold value we set around 2003. We can see that problems of higher education quality evaluation attracted the attention of Chinese scholars after 2003, and this may have been closely related to the Ministry of Education starting the first round of undergraduate education evaluations in 2003. During the second literature review using the keywords "education evaluation" and "quality evaluation" as subjects, the related research mainly concentrated on introducing the background, systems, and experiences of foreign education evaluation or quality evaluation and reflecting on problems existing in Chinese education evaluation. The third main node of this cluster was "quality standards," which appeared around 2006. "Quality standards" is an internal basis for quality evaluation indicator systems, as the quality standards determine what kind of indicator system you have and lead to corresponding quality evaluation and assurance results (Cai and Chen 2013). We can see that after 2006, academic research of higher education quality assessment started turning from the external policy environment to reviewing the internal basis. "Bologna Process" and "student participation" were at the far right of this cluster, and the two were connected by a thick yellow line, meaning that they had a strong co-word relationship during the 2009–11 period. The second literature analysis found that the Bologna Process that was aimed at facilitating unification of European higher education not only clearly advocated student participation and higher education quality assurance in policies, but also provided principles and specific indicators for student participation and quality assurance. Therefore, after 2010, how to implement student participation and mechanisms in the education evaluations of all European countries became a new hot topic of higher education "quality evaluation."

"Teaching management" was the fourth main cluster, and included nine nodes such as "teaching quality," "teaching management," "teaching reform," and "teaching evaluation." Of these, "teaching quality" is the largest node, and it links "teaching management" with the two main clusters of "education reform" and "talent cultivation." We can see that this cluster is a part of the problem of teaching management and reforms that improves "teaching quality." From the timeline in Figure 4 we can see that the discussion of this topic was more intense before 2005, and it clearly cooled off afterward.

The fifth and sixth main clusters were "talent cultivation" and "quality view," and each had six nodes. Figure 3 shows that in the "talent cultivation" cluster, "talent cultivation" is the largest node and is connected to the "education reform" cluster. The most recent high-frequency keywords in this cluster are "improving quality" and "intensive development" that appeared after 2011. The second literature review found that the sudden appearance of these two keywords was directly related to the "Education Plan Outline" mentioning "establishing a view of education development with improving quality as its core, focusing on intensive development of education, and encouraging schools to be unique and of better quality," and many papers that include these two keywords were based on the spirit of the "Educational Plan Outline."

In the "quality view" cluster, "higher education massification" and "higher education quality view" were the largest nodes, and based on the colors of these two large nodes, they set off heated discussions among scholars during the 2000–02 period. The views of Pan (2000), Zhang (2001), and Cai (2001) formed the basic views on higher education quality during the massification phase: giving up the traditional views of elite education quality, establishing developmental, diverse, comprehensive views of higher education quality, and guiding and encouraging different types of schools to develop unique features. But diversity does not mean being haphazard and there must be quality standards. It simply means setting different quality standards for different types of higher education institutions. This recognition constitutes a precondition for Chinese scholars discussing the problems of higher education quality assurance, evaluation, and control in the massification phase. Therefore, there is an extremely clear connecting line between the "higher education quality view" node and "quality assurance."

On the whole, the keyword co-word and cluster analysis shows that in the past 15 years, Chinese research on higher education quality was guided and promoted by implementing the national policies of the strategy of rejuvenating the nation through science and education and the comprehensive and deep education reforms. Under the background of higher education massification, scholars were primarily focused on the subjects of how to change conceptions and form correct views of higher education quality and how to strengthen education management to assure teaching quality and implement talent cultivation objectives. These were closely followed by the problems of assuring and evaluating higher education quality. Related research underwent an evolution from stressing external assurances to advocating an organic integration of the external and internal assurances, from stressing macropolicies and mechanism building to exploring formation of concrete quality standards, and from stressing the role of government and higher education institutions to stressing student participation and valuing evaluations of student learning results.

LEADING TRENDS IN 15 YEARS OF RESEARCH ON CHINESE HIGHER EDUCATION QUALITY

In CiteSpace, leading research is reflected in the burst terms or burst term clusters used in texts forming the text co-citation matrix and their cited texts (Chen et al. 2014). This can be regarded

TABLE 2
Keywords with the Greatest Prominence Rate

Keywords	Prominence rates	Word frequencies	Cluster
Teaching quality	25.19	198	3
Education evaluation	13.56	46	2
Talent cultivation quality	12.63	52	1
Improving quality	8.84	20	4
Quality assurance	7.07	188	0
Education reform	6.88	47	1
Teaching evaluation	6.43	30	3

as a potential research trend in a certain field that suddenly surges during a certain time but is still not stable. CiteSpace's burst term measurement function and the citation history curve provided clearly reflect which topics suddenly became leading research in which periods and their subsequent development trends.

Table 2 provides the seven keywords in the above six main clusters with the highest prominence rates (6.0 and above), word frequencies, and cluster. Figure 5 and Figure 6 are leading history curves of declining and increasing research created by Excel based on the citation history curve graphs of these seven burst terms from CiteSpace.

Figure 5 shows that "teaching quality" and "education reform" were leading subjects that came to prominence in 2000–02 and subsequently had weaker research trends. "Teaching quality" was the keyword with the greatest prominence rate, and during the two periods of 2000–02 and 2003–05, 60 articles were published with these keywords, while this sharply fell to 28 articles in 2006–08, 30 articles in 2009–11, and only 20 articles in 2012–14. This is completely consistent with the development trend of the "education management" cluster that contains teaching quality in the aforementioned timeline. A total of forty seven articles on "education reform" were published, of which nineteen appeared in 2000–02, and this sharply fell to four articles from 2003 to 05. The issuance of the two reform documents, 2006 "11th Five-Year Plan

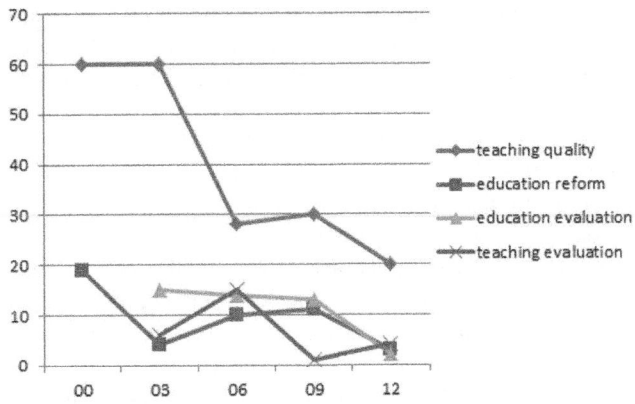

FIGURE 5 Leading history curve of decreasingly popular research (graph: blue—teaching quality, red—education reform, green—education evaluation, purple—teaching evaluation).

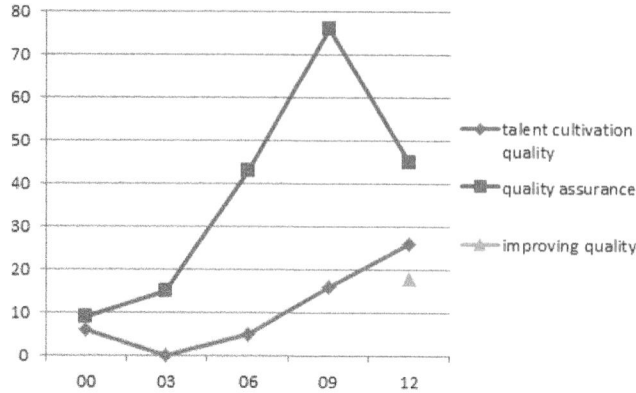

FIGURE 6 Leading history curve of increasingly popular research (graph: blue—talent cultivation quality, red—quality assurance, green—improving quality).

Outline" and 2010 "Education Plan Outline," caused an increase in articles with this keyword from 2006 to 08 and from 2009 to 11, with 10 and 11 articles, respectively, but after 2012 the frequencies of this keyword clearly fell, and during those three years only three articles were published.

"Education evaluation" and "teaching evaluation" were leading subjects that became prominent in 2003–2005 and subsequently had weaker research trends. From 2003 to 2005, 15 articles were published with the keyword "education evaluation," and from 2006 to 2008 and from 2009 to 2011 fourteen and thirteen articles were respectively published, but during the three years from 2012 to 2014, there were only two articles with education evaluation as a keyword. This may be closely related to the Ministry of Education holding its first round of undergraduate education evaluations that started in 2003 and ended in 2008. This was also the reason that the phrase "teaching evaluation" appeared in 2003–2005 with six related articles, and this leapt to fifteen articles in 2006–2008, and sharply fell to one article in 2009–2011. In 2011, drawing on the lessons from the first round of evaluations that "evaluation standards are uniform and have poor differentiation" and "evaluation bodies are uniform and overly administrative," referring to the research results on international experiences with higher education evaluations, the Ministry of Education published a new "Opinions on Undergraduate Education Evaluation Work of General Higher Education Institutions" and proposed a basic framework of "establishing and perfecting an educational evaluation system corresponding to the higher education system with Chinese characteristics, on the basis of institutions' self-evaluations, with the main content of institution evaluations, professional accreditation and evaluation, international evaluations, and regular monitoring of basic teaching data, and combining diverse assessments from governments, institutions, and professional organizations and society" (Liu 2012). Therefore, the number of articles on "education evaluation" slightly increased again in 2012–2014, and related research was mainly concentrated on analyzing and discussing various university self-evaluation reports.

Figure 6 shows that "talent cultivation quality" and "quality assurance" were leaders of increasingly popular research over the past 15 years. From 2000 to 2002 six articles discussed "talent cultivation quality," there were none from 2003 to 2005, then from 2006 to 2008 the number of such articles rose back to five, then from 2009 to 2011 it leapt to sixteen, and further increased to 26 in 2012 and after. The second literature analysis found that the sharp increase in this subject in recent years was closely related to the "Education Plan Outline" and 2012 "Several Opinions of Ministry of Education on Comprehensively Improving the Quality of Higher Education" (hereinafter "Several Opinions") that emphasized "talent cultivation quality" several times. Related discussions were mainly concentrated on specific issues of talent cultivation mechanisms such as practical education, curriculum construction, production-learning cooperation, and entrepreneurial education. The issue of higher education "quality assurance (guarantee)" was discussed many times from 2000 to 2002, and relevant research gradually increased thereafter. The true jump occurred during the periods of 2006–08 and 2009–11, with 43 and 76 articles, respectively. The number fell after 2012, but still remained at the high volume of 45 articles.

"Improving quality" was a burst term that newly appeared from 2012 to 2014, and there were 18 articles with this keyword in these three years alone. A search for articles with the keyword "improve quality" and in-depth reading shows that in 2010 the "Education Plan Outline" was issued, in 2011 General Secretary of China Hu Jintao gave a speech on the hundredth anniversary of Tsinghua University, and in 2012 "Several Opinions" came out, and the successive appearance of these documents caused the phrase "improving quality" to became a burst term after 2012. We can see that as Zhou Yuanqing, President of the China Association of Higher Education, pointed out in his keynote address on the "2011 International Forum on Higher Education," after Chinese higher education underwent major system and concept reforms and major developments in size and structure at the turn of the century, we have entered a period of greatly improving quality and levels today (Zhou 2011). We can anticipate that the subject of higher education quality assurance will be followed by more attention to higher education quality improvement. But looking at current research, most papers on "improving quality" are leadership speeches or superficial promotional slogans, so the problem of how to use truly effective education reforms and curriculum construction to truly improve higher education quality should be a focus of research going forward.

CONCLUSIONS

Through a keyword co-occurrence and cluster analysis and burst term exploration of research articles on Chinese higher education quality over the past 15 years we can find that research on the quality of Chinese higher education was very clearly oriented toward policy and a good interactive relationship was formed between research and policy. The release of each major educational reform document by the Ministry of Education would stimulate the appearance of corresponding research topics on higher education quality, and reflective research on problems appearing in the reforms would facilitate the release of better policies. The release of the new "Opinions of Ministry of Education on Undergraduate Education Evaluation Work of General Higher Education Institutions" was a result of the good interaction between research and policy.

Looking at research topics, apart from macrodiscussions of the spirit of several educational reforms, research topics on Chinese higher education quality are mainly focused on five aspects: higher education quality issues in the massification stage, issues of higher education teaching management and student cultivation, and issues of ensuring and evaluating higher education quality.

Of these, higher education quality issues in the massification stage and issues of higher education academic management and student cultivation were widely discussed by academics from 2000 to 2002, but this focus gradually weakened after that. These topics became a new point of discussion only after 2010 when a series of new education reform documents were released and included for example "improving quality" and "intensive development." These points of discussion may become hot topics in the coming stage of research on higher education quality, but related research urgently needs to move from superficial promotion of slogans to truly feasible plans. Unlike the first three types of topics, the issue of assuring and evaluating higher education quality has continually been in a state of stable research growth, and became the mainstream of research on Chinese higher education quality for the past 15 years. With the 2011 release of "Opinions of Ministry of Education on Undergraduate Education Evaluation Work of General Higher Education Institutions," the issues of how to guide higher education institutions to perform effective self-evaluations and how to truly realize the unification of diverse evaluations from governments, schools, professional organizations, and society will become hot topics of research on ensuring and evaluating higher education quality in the future.

REFERENCES

Cai, K. 2001. Dazhonghua de zhiliangguan: duoyangxing he tongyixing jiehe [A look at the quality of massification: A union of diversity and uniformity]. *Gaodeng jiaoyu yanjiu [Research on Higher Education]* (04).

Cai, Z., and Y. Chen. 2013. Gaodeng jiaoyu zhiliang: Gainian neihan yu zhiliang biaozhun [Quality of higher education: Meaning of concepts and quality standards]. *Qinghua daxue jiaoyu yanjiu [Tsinghua Journal of Education]* (03).

Chen, Y., C. Chen, Z. Hu, and X. Wang. 2014. *Yinwen kongjian fenxi yuanli yu yingyong: CiteSpace shiyong zhinan [Principles and applications of spatial analysis of quotations: CiteSpace practical guidelines]*. Beijing: Kexue chubanshe, 16.

Huang, H. 2013. Meiguo gaoxiao 'xuesheng xuexi chengguo pinggu' de lishi jinzhan [The historical progress of "evaluating student learning results" in American higher education]. *Waiguo jiaoyu yanjiu [Studies in Foreign Education]* (07).

Li, H., X. Zhang, and W. Luo. 2008. 'Gaodeng jiaoyu zhiliang baozhang' yu 'gaodeng jiaoyu zhiliang baozheng' zhi gaonian bianxi [An analysis of the concepts of "assuring the quality of higher education" and "guaranteeing the quality of higher education"]. *Xiangtan daxue xuebao [Journal of Xiangtan University]* (05).

Liu, Z. 2012. Woguo xinyilun gaoxiao benke jiaoxue pinggu zongti sheji yu zhidu chuangxin [The overall design and systemic innovations of the latest round of college undergraduate education evaluations in China]. *Gaodeng jiaoyu yanjiu* (03).

Liu, Z., and W. Wu. 2014. Jiyu CNKI gao beiyin wenzhang de gaodeng jiaoyu zhiliang yanjiu fazhan shitai fenxi [An analysis of the state of development of highly-cited CNKI research papers on the quality of higher education]. *Xiandai jiaoyu kexue [Modern Education Science]* (06).

Pan, L., and S. Wang. 2011. Jin shinianlai jiaoyu yanjiu de redian lingyu he qianyan zhuti [Hot topic areas and leading topics in educational research in the past decade]. *Jiaoyu yanjiu [Educational Research]* (02).

Pan, M. 2000. Gaodeng jiaoyu dazhonghua de jiaoyu zhiliangguan [A look at education quality of popularized higher education]. *Zhongguo gaojiao yanjiu*, (01).

Qiu, J., and W. Lou. 2013. Woguo gaodeng jiaoyu zhiliang yanjiu de xianzhuang yu fazhan—jiyu jiliangxue de tongji fenxi jieguo [The current state and developments in research on quality of higher education in China—Metrology-based statistical analysis results]. *Hongguan zhiliang yanjiu [Journal of Macro-Quality Research]* (03).

Qiu, J., and Y. Ai. 2013. Woguo gaodeng jiaoyu zhiliang yanjiu lunwen de jiliang fenxi [A quantitative analysis of research papers on the quality of higher education in China]. *Zhongguo gaojiao yanjiu* (02).

Qiu, M. 2002. Dazhonghua gaodeng jiaoyu zhiliang yanjiu zongshu [An overview of research on the quality of popularized higher education]. *Jiangsu gaojiao [Jiangsu Higher Education]* (01).

Qu, Y., and B. Meng. 2008. Dazhonghua Beijing xia woguo gaodeng jiaoyu zhiliang yanjiu zongshu [An overview of research on the quality of higher education in China under the background of massification]. *Heilongjiang gaojiao yanjiu [Heilongjiang Higher Education Research]* (06).

Wu, X., and X. Chen. 2012. Guoneiwai gaodeng jiaoyu zhiliang yanjiu de xinjinzhan [New advancements in research on the quality of higher education in China and the world]. *Gaodeng like jiaoyu [Higher Education of Sciences]* (01).

Yan, Z. 2011. 20 shiji 70 niandaimo yilai woguo gaodeng jiaoyu zhiliang yanjiu de huigu yu zhanwang [A look back at research on the quality of higher education in China since the 1970s and future prospects]. *Taiyuan daxue jiaoyu xueyuan xuebao [Journal of Education Institute of Taiyuan University]* (01).

Zhang, Y. 2001. Gaodeng jiaoyu zhiliangguan yu gaodeng jiaoyu dazhonghua Jincheng [A look at higher education quality and progress of higher education massification]. *Jiangsu gaojiao* (05).

Zhou, Y. 2011. Tigao zhiliang shi jiaoyu gaige fazhan de guanjian [Improving quality is the key to education reforms and development]. *Zhongguo gaojiao yanjiu* (11).

Index